The Arno Press Cinema Program

JAMES AGEE:
A Study of His Film Criticism

John J. Snyder

ARNO PRESS

A New York Times Company

New York / 1977

This volume was selected for the
Dissertations on Film Series
of the ARNO PRESS CINEMA PROGRAM
by Garth S. Jowett, University of
Windsor, Canada

Editorial Supervision: Leslie Ike

First publication in book form, 1977,
by Arno Press Inc.

Reprinted from a copy in the St. John's University
Library

THE ARNO PRESS CINEMA PROGRAM
For complete listing of cinema titles see last pages

Manufactured in the United States of America

Library of Congress Cataloging in Publication Data

Snyder, John J   1934-
   James Agee : a study of his film criticism.

   (The Arno Press cinema program) (Dissertations on
film series)
   Revision of the author's thesis, St. John's University,
New York, 1969.
   Bibliography: p.
   1. Agee, James, 1909-1955--Knowledge--
Performing arts. 2. Moving-pictures--Aesthetics.
I. Series. II. Series: Dissertations on film series.
PS3501.G35Z89   1977   791.43   76-40793
ISBN 0-405-09895-2

JAMES AGEE: A STUDY OF HIS FILM CRITICISM

A dissertation submitted in partial
fulfillment of the requirements
for the degree of
   DOCTOR OF PHILOSOPHY

to the faculty of the department of
   ENGLISH

at

St. John's University
New York

by

John J. Snyder

ACKNOWLEDGMENT

Grateful acknowledgment is made to Grosset and Dunlap, Inc.,
for permission to quote from Agee on Film.

To my wife Charlene

TABLE OF CONTENTS

NOTE: Chapter IV was written as a
part of the original dissertation
but was withdrawn, at the last hour,
from the final version. At the request
of the author, it is included here in
its original form. The Introduction
and Bibliography have been altered
only to the extent necessitated by
the addition of this chapter.

INTRODUCTION

Restless, introspective, relatively unknown during his lifetime,
James Agee after death has earned critical respect and a popularity
which has the dimensions of a cult. Born in Knoxville, Tennessee, in
1909, proud to refer to his "hillbilly" blood, he eventually graduated
from Exeter and Harvard to the New York literary life. As a young boy,
he entered St. Andrew's School, where he met the Episcopalian priest,
Fr. Flye, who was to become his dearest, oldest friend, and one of the
few stabilizing influences in his life. At Harvard, Agee edited the
university's literary magazine, The Advocate, and, as a result of a
parody issue of Time magazine, he was offered a job as a cub reporter
for Fortune. Later, he became a staff writer, working on topics as
varied as the Saratoga racing mystique and the orchid industry. In
1941, he began writing unsigned film reviews for Time. In 1942, he
was given complete editorial freedom for a signed film column in The
Nation.

Agee is the only American film critic who, by virtue of his non-
critical writings, can be considered an artist. His poetic tract
Let Us Now Praise Famous Men (1941) has the stature of a minor, if
ragged, American classic. The novel A Death in the Family (1957) was
awarded a Pulitzer Prize posthumously. The short novel The Morning
Watch (1951); his collection of poetry Permit Me Voyage, originally
published in 1934 and re-issued in 1968; and his film and television
scripts, notably The African Queen (1951) and Abraham Lincoln - The
Early Years (1952), are respectable achievements. His letters to Fr.

Flye, published in 1962, have also contributed to his literary reputation.

For this relatively small body of work, representing the effort of some twenty-five years, Agee has received abundant praise. Dwight Macdonald in 1967 expressed the belief that he was "the most copiously talented writer of my generation."[1] In 1966, John Simon wrote that there are probably only three modern American writers who, caught up in legends and cults, have become myths: Fitzgerald, Hemingway, and Agee. He added that Agee's posthumous reputation was spreading steadily, even fanatically.[2]

This versatile, restless writer became a critic, not for economic reasons, but because of a love for films. When asked if Agee reviewed films as a means for supporting his "creative writing," Fr. Flye replied with a brief story. On the day of their return to New York from a summer tour in Europe in 1925, Agee, fifteen years old, asked if they could see F. W. Murnau's The Last Laugh, which he had heard was playing somewhere in Brooklyn. After searching for some time in a taxi, they lighted upon the particular movie house. Agee admired the film thoroughly and continued to discuss it for hours with his beloved, but at that point, very tired friend. Fr. Flye's meaning was that Agee always had an enthusiasm for films, and was later pleased that he

[1]
"Agee and the Movies," Film Heritage, III (Fall 1967), 3-11.

[2]
"Exemplary Failure," New York Times Book Review, August 14, 1966, p. 2.

had the opportunity of reviewing them.[3]

On the strength of eight years of distinguished film reviewing, from 1941 to 1948, Agee ranks as one of the foremost American film critics. An entire issue of Film Heritage (Fall, 1967) is devoted to him, and although some are little more than vapid eulogies, the articles collectively assert that his position as a film critic has been unequalled in America. Pauline Kael thinks that the only film critic comparable to him in sensibility and intelligence is André Bazin of France.[4] Manny Farber accounts for Agee's achievement as a critic by citing his notable influence, claiming that "he set up a hailstorm of ideas for other critics to use."[5] Joel Siegel states that any young film critic practicing today must acknowledge some debt to Agee.[6] Considering Agee's entire career, Dwight Macdonald views the criticism from an interesting perspective:

> Earlier he might have developed his literary
> talents without distraction from cinema;
> later on he could have made movies like
> everybody else, On-Hollywood or Off-Hollywood
> [sic]. As it was, he had to settle for
> writing about movies instead of directing them.

[3] This information was obtained during an interview with Fr. Flye in New York City on January 9, 1968.

[4] I Lost It at the Movies (Boston, 1966), p. 266.

[5] "Star-Gazing for the Middlebrows," New Leader, XLI (December 8, 1958), 14-15.

[6] "On 'Agee on Film'," Film Heritage, III (Fall 1967), 12-19.

Not so bad for us, not so good for him.[7]

Although I do not accept the idea that Agee had to settle for criticism as something second-best, I can appreciate the spirit of Macdonald's back-handed compliment.

In this dissertation, Agee's esthetic is viewed in various con-texts. It is compared and contrasted with the theories and practices of other critics, theorists, and film-makers. The historical develop-ments in cinematic theory and practice, which took place before and after Agee's tenure as movie reviewer, are also examined. Finally, Agee's criticism is placed in a context of his entire non-critical writings, from the earlier Fortune articles to the script of Noa-Noa, one of his last works.

Agee's esthetic is not systematized, since he was writing reviews of specific films for periodicals, not a book of film theory. No attempt was made to impose a coherent system on the criticism. It was necessary to expand, explain, or interpret Agee's critical position throughout the disseration, because he does not always define or specify his criteria in the articles, and because his style is journalistic, and frequently impressionistic.

The first chapter examines Agee's understanding of the film medium. He treats its range, power, and uniqueness of communication. The film can convey a feeling of immediacy, actuality, and spontaneity. Its tense is the present. Agee compares and contrasts the film with other art forms, in particular the novel, the stage play, music, and painting. This chapter also considers his concepts in the light of the Kracauer

---

[7] "Agee and the Movies," Film Heritage, III (Fall 1967), 3-11.

controversy over the nature of the film. Because of its foundation in photography, is the film wedded to a strict form of realism, or, because of its spatial and temporal freedom, is it more amenable to fantasy? Finally the chapter deals with what Agee considered the most unfavorable conditions affecting the medium during the 1940's, his period of reviewing: Hollywood, in its pejorative connotation; the Motion Picture Production Code; and the general movie audience.

Agee's preference for a style most suited to the film medium is the subject of Chapter II. He elects to merge the two fundamental but divergent modes, realism and fantasy. Because of its foundation in photography, the film can establish a convincing form of realism. In itself, however, realism can smother as readily as it can liberate any feeling of reality. The Italian neo-realism of the 1940's, with its documentary format, was close in practice to Agee's concept of poetic realism, but he envisions the great film as embodying more of the essence of poetry. Any form of indirect discourse, like allegory or fantasy, must have a solid foundation in realism for screen presentation. Agee also prefers films which have a sense of motion and a visual quality. A film is the telling of a story primarily by visual means. Cinema's first law is to keep the images moving; yet Agee dismisses motion for motion's sake. In the integration of realism, poetry, motion, and the visual, the film can achieve its most effective style.

Chapter III is a study of Agee's treatment of film techniques. He is too much the humanist to stress the mechanics more than the content of a film. His priorities are clear: theme, character, story, setting, style. Yet his interest in, and knowledge of, a

motion picture camera and of editing had much to do in making his
reviews, in the words of Gerald Weales, the most perceptive
accounts of pure "seeing" that film criticism has to offer.[8]   Agee
insists on the use of actual locations, instead of studio sets, because
of the camera's power to record faithfully the external world. His
arguments, extending over a period of eight years, were opposed by
many producers and critics for both commercial and esthetic reasons.
In the late 1960's, location-shooting has become a standard operating
procedure. Of all the technical areas of the film treated in this
chapter, sound is the most controversial. Though an ardent admirer
of silent film, Agee was one of the few earlier critics who whole-
heartedly endorsed the use of sound.

His acceptance of color was not as immediate, though an
appreciation grew as the process was perfected. Initially, he dismissed
color as a gimmick, great for "lipsticky kisses." Years later, he
realized that its proper use could make raw reality even rawer. In
opposition to most of his contemporaries, and many critics of the 1960's,
he argued that color could be as effective for stark, realistic dramas
as for splashy, romantic musicals. In this instance of an endorsement
of color for all kinds of films, his hailstorm of ideas has not yet
widely penetrated the film community.

_____

[8]
"The Critic in Love," Reporter, XIX (December 25, 1958), 38-39.

Chapter IV has an entirely different focus: not Agee's esthetic, but his expression of that esthetic. It is concerned with the manner in which he conveys the ideas, judgments and opinions examined in the previous three chapters. There is as much love as anger in the criticism. He loved and was committed to film to a degree that was unfashionable for that period of time; he lashed out angrily, at times savagely, at what he considered the deceptions commonly practiced in Hollywood.

Agee's prose style is in a class by itself. No other prose of an American film critic before or since can be compared. His intuition for the right word is a poet's gift, as was his ease and grace with the use of metaphorical language. He was also blessed with a flowing, Southern rhetoric, though at times it carried him away at high tide. A pervasive, "gashouse" humor keeps the criticism from becoming heavy or dense, like the abstract theorizing of a Bazin.

An abiding, deeply felt morality undergirds the criticism. His commitment to and compassion for mankind at times ran contrary to popular beliefs, as occurred during the Second World War when Agee objected to certain kinds of American propaganda. No matter what the issue or subject under consideration, he was unabashedly subjective. In one review he simply confesses that the only way he knows how to write is subjectively. Because

he was so personal in reacting to each work in front of
him, not relying on some type of critical scale or
formula, his criticism reveals a flexibility and
largeness of spirit. The chapter also examines his
critical judgments in terms of their perception and
influence, with consideration given to how well these
judgments have stood the test of time. In essence,
this final chapter investigates the question of what
are the effects on the style of a body of film criticism
when that criticism has been written by a person as
much a poet and novelist as a critic.

CHAPTER I

THE FILM AS AN ART FORM

Before the sustained, serious work by directors like Bergman,

Antonioni, Fellini, and Godard, many intellectuals tended to dismiss

any notion that the film should be treated as an art form. Throughout

the 1920's and 1930's, movies were generally considered a form of

low entertainment. Unlike the novel or stage play, they were not

accorded serious, critical analysis. This attitude extended into the

1940's and was partly represented by Wolcott Gibbs' public complaint

that, as film critic for The New Yorker, he was in one sense wasting

his time writing film reviews. For years he had addressed them to his

social and intellectual peers, but discovered, unhappily, that they
                                          1
were being read only by their cooks.

Further evidence of the status of movies is W. H. Auden's letter

to the editors of The Nation in 1944, two years after Agee began

reviewing films for that magazine. In praising the "astonishing

excellence" of Agee's film column, Auden incidentally revealed his

attitude toward the film.

> In my opinion, his column is the most remarkable
> regular event in American journalism today. What
> he says is of such profound interest, expressed
> with such extraordinary wit and felicity, and so
> transcends its ostensible -- to me, rather

1
    "The Kingdom of the Blind," Saturday Review of Literature,
XXVIII (November 17, 1945), 7-8.

> unimportant -- subject, that his articles belong
> in that very select class -- the music critiques
> of Berlioz and Shaw are the only other members I
> know -- of newspaper work which has permanent
> literary value.

Concerning this "unimportant subject," Auden frankly admitted in the

same letter that he did not care for movies very much and rarely saw

them.[2] Such a statement by an artist and critic about any recognized

major art form would have constituted an admission of weakness or

blindness; since Auden wrote it in the 1940's about "movies," it

demonstrated the taste and sensibility expected of a man in his

position.

James Agee opposed the general intellectual tenor of the times

by admiring movies, without condescension or patronage. Even though

he was often enthusiastic about the potential of the film, he never

resorted to the "coterie cuteness about art cinema."[3] Laurence

Olivier's 1946 film version of Henry V amounted to either a violation,

a simplification, or a sense-bludgeoning rendition of Shakespeare

to some reviewers. Agee declared that Shakespeare shone in new

splendor as a result of the collaboration of artists who achieved

some of the promise of "this vital, new medium" (36). In an article

---

[2] *Agee on Films: Reviews and Comments* (New York, 1958), introduction. All further references, which will be set in parentheses within the text, are to this edition. There is a substantial and highly significant amount of criticism not collected in the *Agee on Film* volume: 120 film reviews, dating from September 7, 1942, to January 26, 1948, and over 130 book and theater reviews, dating from January 1, 1940, to May 19, 1947, all written for *Time* Magazine. I have relied heavily in the dissertation on this untapped and unexamined source.

[3] Gerald Weales, "The Critic in Love," *Reporter*, XX (December 25, 1958), 38.

on John Huston he hailed the cinema as "the greatest art medium of
the century" (321). These exuberant claims must be considered in the
context of his judgment, made in 1944, that movies stand up
surprisingly well compared to the books published, the pictures
painted, and the music composed during a given year (136). Because
such sweeping declarations of praise punctuate Agee's criticism, Jack
Behar accuses him of sounding at times too much like "an obsessed
critic."[4] I believe that he was obsessed, but not to his discredit,
with the conviction that the film medium represents the greatest
prospect for a major popular art since the days of the Elizabethan
theatre.

Although this outlook separated Agee from many intellectuals of
his day, he was in the select company of men who, from the first two
decades of this century, have recognized the revolutionary impact
film can have on man's understanding of the world. The Hungarian
critic Béla Balázs, writing in 1923 when the silent film was at the
zenith of its development in Germany, claimed that once again man has
become visible because of the film. The new visual dimensions
introduced by the medium of film would be as revolutionary to the
print-dominated man of the twentieth century as was the introduction
of print to the visually-dominated man of the fifteenth century.[5]

---

[4] "James Agee: The World of His Work" (Ann Arbor, 1963), p.96. An
unpublished dissertation from Ohio State University.

[5] Theory of Film, trans. Edith Bone (New York, 1953), p. 40. The
Columbia Broadcasting System recently developed a machine the size of
a bread basket, which, when attached to the top of a T.V. set, can
project feature-length sound films through the set. This invention,
when marketed in 1970, will make possible an individual's acquiring a
"visual library" of movie tapes, similar to a library of books.

René Clair in 1926 asserted that a spectator becomes a dreamer under
the spell of a movie, which not only enables a suspension of disbelief,
but also encourages a form of partial self-hypnosis. James Joyce, who
experimented with the medium of print to a degree not yet surpassed in
the twentieth century, foresaw the staggering effects film would have
on man's senses, his language, and his thought processes. He believed,
like Clair, that illusion and fantasy are so potent in the film that
society was being transformed into an "allnights newseryreel."[6]
Because man's view of the world was being filtered through a filmic
image, his concepts of the temporal and spatial dimensions would
become more relative. Within this context, Joyce proclaimed that the
film was no longer just a rival but a usurper of the word and would
ultimately bring about "the abnihilisation of the etym."[7]

In their grasp of the revolutionary implications of the film
medium, these men, as well as a few others like Sergei Eisenstein and
V.I. Pudovkin, anticipated by some thirty years the present interest
in the electronic media. Generated principally by Marshall McLuhan,
attention has centered on the effect of the media. Agee's film
reviews of the 1940's, written some ten years prior to McLuhan's
"probings," reveal a significant similarity with the findings now
being published. The central pronouncement of McLuhan is that the
medium is the message.

---

[6] James Joyce, _Finnegan's Wake_ (New York, 1939), p. 489.

[7] James Joyce, _Finnegan's Wake_ (New York, 1939), p. 353.

> This is merely to say that the personal and social
> consequences of any medium -- that is, of any
> extension of ourselves -- result from the new scale
> that is introduced into our affairs by each [8]
> extension of ourselves, or by any new technology.

McLuhan warns that any medium has the power of affecting a person

without his being aware of it. A spell can occur instantly upon

contact between image and audience, just as can happen in an audience's

hearing the first bars of a melody. He laments that literate man, in

not being attuned to the discontinuous simultaneous flow of images of

the electronic media, has not heeded William Blake's warning that man

becomes what he beholds.[9] To some degree man has always been shaped

and conditioned by the dominant elements in his environment. Today,

the electronic media are surely among the environmental "messages."

Agee in the 1940's grasped the extent of the film medium's

message. He reported that the 1948 The Iron Curtain divulged much

less about Communist front groups than the daily press had already

revealed. Of the groups who protested and picketed the showing of

this film, on the ground that it disclosed too much information, Agee

wrote, "yet the alarm and breast-beating of the opposition are an

understandable tribute to the enormous and unique power of motion

picture propaganda in general."[10] Mission to Moscow, a Hollywood

propaganda effort made during the Second World War to strengthen the

United States' ties with the Soviet Union, prompted Agee to declare

---

[8]
Understanding Media: The Extensions of Man (New York, 1964), p. 7.

[9]
Understanding Media: The Extensions of Man (New York, 1964), p.19.

[10]"The New Pictures," Time, LI (May 17,1948), 102-106. Unsigned
review by Agee.

that the cinema's powers for good or evil, enlightenment or deceit, were appalling (37). A film successful in achieving a good deal of the medium's potential was The Raider, which forced audiences to live vicariously through the experience of surviving in a lifeboat: the swollen features, the livid coloring, the feebleness of motion, and the crushing headache were all communicated forcefully enough "to hurt an audience, and hurt it badly" (224). Agee, then, was aware of the potential revolutionary impact of film that Balázs and Joyce had perceived years before, and that McLuhan has since popularized.

Agee's film script for The Quiet One in the 1940's, and his five published film scripts, written in the early 1950's, reveal that he was able not only to theorize about the medium, but in practice to experiment with some of its resources. The adaptation of the African Queen is an instance of a film maker in control of his medium. Noa-Noa and the Blue Hotel in particular demonstrate a mastery of some of the intricacies of the film.[11] For the script, Abraham Lincoln - The Early Years, Agee successfully applied knowledge of the film medium to the more intimate expression of television.[12]

The special qualities of the film as a communication medium are defined in terms of uniqueness, density, and simultaneity. In one of the later reviews, Agee contends that the film is "unique as a recorder of actual existence."[13] Handled correctly, the film can

---

[11] See Behar, pp. 114-187, for a separate, adequate analysis of each of the five scripts.

[12] Meyer Levin, "Abraham Lincoln Through the Picture Tube," Reporter, VIII (April 14, 1953), 31-33.

[13] "Farrebique," Time, LII (March 15, 1948), 100-104.

perceive, record, and communicate with stunning power a segment of
reality (297). The motion picture camera, one of the advanced tools
of technology, achieves a representation of the external world with a
degree of fidelity previously unattainable. Agee believed throughout
his career as book reviewer and theater critic, as poet and novelist,
that the film, of all art forms, least diminishes reality in the
process of its transference to an audience. Yet he demands more of a
film than a stenographic transcription of reality: great cinema, like
Vittorio da Sica's Shoeshine, achieves a dimension beyond the real.

André Malraux's Man's Hope communicates superbly the density and
specificity in the flow of reality. A night drive through deep country
in order to locate automobiles needed to head-light the bombers'
take-off illustrates film's ability to handle both inner emotions
and external circumstances. In Agee's judgment, "the hypnosis,
exhaustion, sadness, and beauty of such a task, and the passage of
hours, are utterly communicated, not just comfortably suggested" (241).
In the same manner, McLuhan has called attention to the "sheer quantity
of data" that can be contained in a single shot in a film.[14] This same
dense communication occurs in John Huston's "San Pietro," which Agee
considers the finest film record of the Second World War.

> No war film I have seen has been quite so attentive
> to the heaviness of casualties, and to the number
> of yards gained or lost, in such an action; none has
> so levelly watched and implied what it meant, in
> such full and complex terms -- in military terms;
> in terms of the men who were doing the fighting;
> in terms of the villagers; and of their village;

[14] McLuhan, p. 288.

and of the surrounding country; and of the
natural world; and of human existence and hope
(163).

Marshall McLuhan describes the film medium as "hot": it contains
such a high information level that the audience has little to fill in
or to complete. In this sense, there is low participation or
"completion" on the part of the viewer. Television, by contrast, is
described as "cool." Because of television's limited power to convey
density and quantity of data, the viewer has to fill in the image.[15]
Agee notes this power of the medium particularly in war documentaries.
"The Fighting Lady" heaps astonishments "so quickly upon one another
that eye and mind can hardly keep pace."[16] The same film shown on
television would not have a comparably "hot" or staggering impact. The
nature of the medium determines in part the effect content will have
on audiences.

Speed of communication, in the form of instant information
transferral, is a corollary to the "hot" capacity of the medium. In
the 1947 review of David Lean's Great Expectations, Agee regrets that
more minor characters are not sketched into the background, since "the
screen can communicate in a second or two what may require pages in
print" (267). McLuhan in Understanding Media expresses the same
viewpoint. In contrast to the medium of the printed page, the film can
communicate a bulk of information in seconds: "In an instant it

---

[15]
McLuhan, p. 23.

[16]
"The Fighting Lady," Time, XLV (January 22, 1945), 91-92.

presents a scene of landscape with figures that would require several
pages of prose to describe."[17] Reviewing The Beginning or the End (a
fiction film rushed on to the market by M.G.M. to capitalize on the
emotions aroused by the explosion of the atomic bomb), Agee charges
that it tells incomparably less in two hours of the terror and agony
of the bomb than particular newsreel shots of Hiroshima's surviving
victims told in two minutes.[18] The film fails not because of any
weakness of the medium, but because of inept film-makers.

Simultaneous communication on the screen permits the instant
conveyance of data. Agee was aware of this considerably before he
began reviewing films. In Let Us Now Praise Famous Men, he complained
that words are among the most inaccurate of all media of communication,
because of their "inability to communicate simultaneity with any
immediacy."[19] He asserted further that simultaneity permeates all of
nature, is basic to life, and yet the arts have ignored this
fundamental fact.

> As Canada is retired out of summer, the Argentine
> is restored into summer, as simultaneously, as
> literally, as the edge of night is balanced by
> the edge of day, midnight by noon. Just how much
> poetry, or art, or plain human consciousness, has
> taken this into account. [sic] You have only to

[17] McLuhan, p. 288

[18] "The New Pictures," Time, XLIX (February 24, 1947), 106-110.

[19] Let Us Now Praise Famous Men (Boston, 1960), pp. 236-237.

> look at all the autumn art about death and at all
> the spring art about life to get an idea: we are
> so blindfold [sic] by local fact that we cannot
> even imagine this simultaneity.[20]

Some ten years later, Agee frequently had occasion to note this type of communication in various films. Arctic Passage, concerning the construction of the Alaskan Military Highway, depicts two essential opposites simultaneously: the odds against the workers, their progress north.[21] In McLuhan's terms, the message of the movie medium is "transition from lineal connection to configuration"; it is this which enables the projection of simultaneous events at the same instant.[22] The linear communication of typography demands a reading of words and sentences in sequence, and thus meanings build cumulatively. Of course, within this cumulative building an author (Joyce in Finnegan's Wake) can control time relatively: allow for the merging of past and present in the reader's individual consciousness. Agee argues, however, that this is different from the film's ability to project many things at once, in one simultaneous communication. Because he regularly analyzes this as well as other capacities of the medium, Dwight Macdonald claims justifiably that Agee's film criticism is suffused with intimate understanding.[23] And Bosley Crowther refers to

[20] Let Us Now Praise Famous Men (Boston, 1960), p. 248.

[21] "Arctic Passage," Time, XLII (September 27, 1943), 97.

[22] McLuhan, p. 12.

[23] "Agee and the Movies," Film Heritage, III (Fall 1967), 3-11.

if they had been shot by invisible newsreel cameras" (195). As he
throughout the criticism, Agee relies on his purely subjective
onses to discuss the film's techniques for producing certain effects.
Historically, film-makers have attempted to intensify their films
nveying an impression of spontaneity. D. W. Griffith did not
w a detailed scenario while shooting a film so that, having only
gh mental outline of the action, he could improvise, and thus
a better chance of capturing a feeling of improvisation.[30] Jean
au, during the filming of The Beauty and the Beast, wrote in his
that his production manager complained about falling behind
le. Cocteau mused, "it's these extras, the inspiration of the
, which enliven and enrich a film. . . . But I don't like
up my mind too far ahead. Films gain by improvisation."[31]
even more than in the past, many leading directors, like
ni, Fellini, Godard, and Bresson, are endeavoring to convey
eity by allowing some degree of improvisation in their work.[32]
e names can be added Roman Polanski in Repulsion, Richard
in Petulia, Claude LeLouch in A Man and a Woman, Agnes Varda
nheur, Francois Truffaut in The 400 Blows, and Peter Brook
of the Flies. This partial list does not include the
d camera directors of the American Underground Cinema, who

on, p. 89.

of a Film (New York, 1950), p. 36.

ope Huston, The Contemporary Cinema (Baltimore, 1963), pp.
believes that the extent of this practice points toward a
ma."

Agee's "exceptional sensitivity" to the nature of cinema expression.[24]

In a 1922 documentary, an Eskimo hunter licked an icy blade, and
many in the audience flinched. Agee believes that the greatest
advantage of the film medium is making audiences "see feelingly,"
amply demonstrated by Robert Flaherty in Nanook of the North, one of
the forerunners of the modern realistic film. For the sake of
analysis, Agee's recognition of this capacity for producing mental
tactility (of feeling things in the mind), can be divided into three
areas: the sense of the present tense, immediacy, and spontaneity.
The instant present is the tense of the film. Ideally, a film gives
the impression that what is on the screen is happening at that
precise instant. In Agee's day most of the movies appeared as
"glossy, comfortably researched reenactment at eighty years' remove."
He compares many of these movies to predigested food, since they are
reproductions of something that happened in script preparation. John
Huston is commended as one of the few directors who keep the sense
of the present strong throughout shooting. As a result, his films
have a degree of tension, a sense of beginning and life, rather than
a stale feeling of the finished product (326).

Immediacy, another dimension of the present tense, gives a
spectator the feeling that he is participating in the experience
taking place on the screen at that instant. Describing a war
documentary, Attack! — The Invasion of New Britain, Agee notes the
"petrifying immediacy" that is communicated of a landing barge under

[24] Review of Agee on Film: Reviews and Comments, American Scholar,
XXIX (Summer, 1960), 436.

fire in the Normandy invasion: the crouched soldiers, the standing, almost smiling officer, the housetops of the French shore which appear large and distinct, the abrupt, shocking landing (99). Open City's finest achievement is the conveyance of immediacy. Since the events in it had been recently lived through, many of the actual spots were used, and the film's "spirit is still, scarcely cooled at all, the exalted spirit of the actual experience" (195). "Actuality" is the other term Agee uses interchangeably with immediacy. Any distinction would be academic. In describing the sudden take-off of an airplane, he writes that one can feel the "sudden magical suction in the midriff which the actual experience brings."[25]

In the early 1950's, Agee was able to embody this quality of actuality in his series on Lincoln, acclaimed by many critics to be one of the outstanding achievements in television. The opening death scene is in a documentary style with the narrator precisely recording every movement: "Dr. Taft put his hand over the heart. Dr. Leale held the wrist."[26] In a matter of minutes, the audience is made to feel as though it is living within the experience. The whole work, in the judgment of Meyer Levin, "typifies the sense of intimacy and immediacy which distinguish the Lincoln series at its best."[27]

---

[25] "The New Pictures," Time, XLIII (March 27, 1944), 94-96.

[26] Abraham Lincoln - The Early Years in The Lively Arts, eds. Rodney Sheratsky and John L. Reilly (New York, 1964), p. 380.

[27] "Abraham Lincoln Through the Picture Tube," Reporter, VIII (April 14, 1953), 31-33.

Not all film theorists have concurred with Agee concerning th[e] power of the film to capture immediacy. A. R. Fulton states that characteristic of television which the film can not possess is "immediacy," because time must elapse between filming and projec[tion] while in television the recording and projecting (as in news pro[grams]) can be simultaneous.[28] This distinction seems to be based on t[he] limited perspective of a mechanical, technical difference. The relevant question is whether at the moment of projection there [is] conveyed a sense of immediacy. The immediacy that matters is that which exists before the camera, but the illusion created i[n] mind of the viewer.[29] It is ironic that Agee communicated i[n] television series, more than in any of his film scripts, the [sense] of immediacy which he believed to be the major advantage of [that] medium.

Mental tactility is also produced by a sense of sponta[neity]. Vittorio da Sica achieved this in Shoeshine by having the [cinematic] image on the screen appear unarranged, as though in fact [it were] happening for the first time. For this illusion to be cr[eated, neither] the characters nor their actions can be hovered over for [special] effects. In Open City, the hectic raid on the bakery by [the] semi-hysterical people; the sudden arrest of the priest in mid-day; the court-yard search of all the inhabitant[s of a] tenament by the Nazis, are, to Agee, "as shatteringly [true]

---

[28] Motion Pictures (Oklahoma, 1960), p. 266.

[29] See Ivor Montagu, Film World (Middlesex, 1964), a perceptive treatment of the illusion of reality in

like to claim spontaneity for their films. Most often, any feeling
of spontaneity is destroyed by the distraction of their "natural"
practices.

In the conviction that the film is an art form, Agee regularly
compares and contrasts it with the other arts. Most frequently
discussed are the novel, the stage play, and music. Agee's premise
is that these art forms are distinct, governed by separate aesthetic
laws and conventions. The Confidential Agent, a film version of one
of Graham Greene's "entertainments," is ironically disappointing
because it never leaves the pages of the novel.

> Greene's greatest talent — which is, I think,
> with the look and effluence of places, streets,
> and things — is not once even approximated.
> This is odd, because in these respects Greene
> achieves in print what more naturally belongs
> in films, and in a sense does not write novels
> at all, but verbal movies. I don't entirely like
> to think so, but he may have proved that certain
> kinds of movies anyhow are better on the page
> than they can ever be on the screen. (179)

Conversely, in comparing a Preston Sturges effort with the best of
René Clair's comedies, Agee concludes that the best of domestic and
anarchic satire is too purely cinematic to be suggested in words (343).
Agee could have clarified this concept if he had defined, instead of
only suggesting, the fundamental difference between the novel and the
film: Language is as basic to the novel as photography is to the
film. For this reason, certain subjects which inherently contain a
great deal of movement, like anarchic satire, are more suited to the
dynamic, visual medium of cinema.

More recent film theorists have also expressed the conviction that the film and the novel are distinct aesthetic forms, each shaping and affecting material in its own way. Agee would accept Suzanne Langer's comparison of film with dream in the mode of presentation. In creating a virtual present with direct apparition, the film is not a new technique; it is a new poetic mode. "This is not the mode of fiction, which is 'like' memory, or of drama, which is 'like' action. It is the mode of dream, with the dreamer always at the center of it."[33] Ingmar Bergman distinguishes distinct forms, but less convincingly than Langer. He believes that the novel works primarily through print to the intellect and the will, while the film works through pictures directly to feelings.[34] This statement is ironic in that most films of Bergman, like those of Bunuel and Antonioni, are more static and intellectual than the more visual, emotional films of Kurosawa and Fellini.

George Bluestone argues that ballet, an art in time and motion, is as comparable to the static art of architecture as the film, also a time art, is to the static novel.[35] Interested in establishing the fact of two separate forms, Bluestone does not argue for the superiority of one form over another. The primary principle that

---

[33] "A Note on the Film," in Film: A Montage of Theories, ed. Richard Dyer Mac Cann (New York, 1966), p. 199.

[34] Four Screenplays of Ingmar Bergman, trans. Lars Malrustrom and David Kushner (New York, 1960), p. xviii.

[35] Novels into Films (Berkeley, 1966), p. 5.

Agee's "exceptional sensitivity" to the nature of cinema expression.[24]

In a 1922 documentary, an Eskimo hunter licked an icy blade, and many in the audience flinched. Agee believes that the greatest advantage of the film medium is making audiences "see feelingly," amply demonstrated by Robert Flaherty in Nanook of the North, one of the forerunners of the modern realistic film. For the sake of analysis, Agee's recognition of this capacity for producing mental tactility (of feeling things in the mind), can be divided into three areas: the sense of the present tense, immediacy, and spontaneity. The instant present is the tense of the film. Ideally, a film gives the impression that what is on the screen is happening at that precise instant. In Agee's day most of the movies appeared as "glossy, comfortably researched reenactment at eighty years' remove." He compares many of these movies to predigested food, since they are reproductions of something that happened in script preparation. John Huston is commended as one of the few directors who keep the sense of the present strong throughout shooting. As a result, his films have a degree of tension, a sense of beginning and life, rather than a stale feeling of the finished product (326).

Immediacy, another dimension of the present tense, gives a spectator the feeling that he is participating in the experience taking place on the screen at that instant. Describing a war documentary, Attack! — The Invasion of New Britain, Agee notes the "petrifying immediacy" that is communicated of a landing barge under

Review of Agee on Film: Reviews and Comments, American Scholar, XXIX (Summer, 1960), 436.

fire in the Normandy invasion: the crouched soldiers, the standing, almost smiling officer, the housetops of the French shore which appear large and distinct, the abrupt, shocking landing (99). Open City's finest achievement is the conveyance of immediacy. Since the events in it had been recently lived through, many of the actual spots were used, and the film's "spirit is still, scarcely cooled at all, the exalted spirit of the actual experience" (195). "Actuality" is the other term Agee uses interchangeably with immediacy. Any distinction would be academic. In describing the sudden take-off of an airplane, he writes that one can feel the "sudden magical suction in the midriff which the actual experience brings."[25]

In the early 1950's, Agee was able to embody this quality of actuality in his series on Lincoln, acclaimed by many critics to be one of the outstanding achievements in television. The opening death scene is in a documentary style with the narrator precisely recording every movement: "Dr. Taft put his hand over the heart. Dr. Leale held the wrist."[26] In a matter of minutes, the audience is made to feel as though it is living within the experience. The whole work, in the judgment of Meyer Levin, "typifies the sense of intimacy and immediacy which distinguish the Lincoln series at its best."[27]

[25]
"The New Pictures," Time, XLIII (March 27, 1944), 94-96.

[26]
Abraham Lincoln - The Early Years in The Lively Arts, eds. Rodney Sheratsky and John L. Reilly (New York, 1964), p. 380.

[27]
"Abraham Lincoln Through the Picture Tube," Reporter, VIII (April 14, 1953), 31-33.

Not all film theorists have concurred with Agee concerning the power of the film to capture immediacy. A. R. Fulton states that a characteristic of television which the film can not possess is "immediacy," because time must elapse between filming and projecting, while in television the recording and projecting (as in news programs) can be simultaneous.[28] This distinction seems to be based on the limited perspective of a mechanical, technical difference. The only relevant question is whether at the moment of projection there is conveyed a sense of immediacy. The immediacy that matters is not that which exists before the camera, but the illusion created in the mind of the viewer.[29] It is ironic that Agee communicated in his television series, more than in any of his film scripts, the sense of immediacy which he believed to be the major advantage of the film medium.

Mental tactility is also produced by a sense of spontaneity. Vittorio da Sica achieved this in Shoeshine by having the projected image on the screen appear unarranged, as though in fact it was happening for the first time. For this illusion to be created, neither the characters nor their actions can be hovered over for special effects. In Open City, the hectic raid on the bakery by storming, semi-hysterical people; the sudden arrest of the priest on a street in mid-day; the court-yard search of all the inhabitants of a tenament by the Nazis, are, to Agee, "as shatteringly uninvented-looking

28
Motion Pictures (Oklahoma, 1960), p. 266.

29
See Ivor Montagu, Film World (Middlesex, 1964), pp. 293-295, for a perceptive treatment of the illusion of reality in the film.

as if they had been shot by invisible newsreel cameras" (195). As he does throughout the criticism, Agee relies on his purely subjective responses to discuss the film's techniques for producing certain effects.

Historically, film-makers have attempted to intensify their films by conveying an impression of spontaneity. D. W. Griffith did not follow a detailed scenario while shooting a film so that, having only a rough mental outline of the action, he could improvise, and thus have a better chance of capturing a feeling of improvisation.[30] Jean Cocteau, during the filming of The Beauty and the Beast, wrote in his diary that his production manager complained about falling behind schedule. Cocteau mused, "it's these extras, the inspiration of the moment, which enliven and enrich a film. . . . But I don't like making up my mind too far ahead. Films gain by improvisation."[31] Today, even more than in the past, many leading directors, like Antonioni, Fellini, Godard, and Bresson, are endeavoring to convey spontaneity by allowing some degree of improvisation in their work.[32] To these names can be added Roman Polanski in Repulsion, Richard Lester in Petulia, Claude LeLouch in A Man and a Woman, Agnes Varda in Le Bonheur, Francois Truffaut in The 400 Blows, and Peter Brook in Lord of the Flies. This partial list does not include the hand-held camera directors of the American Underground Cinema, who

---

[30] Fulton, p. 89.

[31] Diary of a Film (New York, 1950), p. 36.

[32] Penelope Huston, The Contemporary Cinema (Baltimore, 1963), pp. 188-190, believes that the extent of this practice points toward a "new cinema."

like to claim spontaneity for their films. Most often, any feeling

of spontaneity is destroyed by the distraction of their "natural"

practices.

In the conviction that the film is an art form, Agee regularly

compares and contrasts it with the other arts. Most frequently

discussed are the novel, the stage play, and music. Agee's premise

is that these art forms are distinct, governed by separate aesthetic

laws and conventions. The Confidential Agent, a film version of one

of Graham Greene's "entertainments," is ironically disappointing

because it never leaves the pages of the novel.

> Greene's greatest talent — which is, I think,
> with the look and effluence of places, streets,
> and things — is not once even approximated.
> This is odd, because in these respects Greene
> achieves in print what more naturally belongs
> in films, and in a sense does not write novels
> at all, but verbal movies. I don't entirely like
> to think so, but he may have proved that certain
> kinds of movies anyhow are better on the page
> than they can ever be on the screen. (179)

Conversely, in comparing a Preston Sturges effort with the best of

René Clair's comedies, Agee concludes that the best of domestic and

anarchic satire is too purely cinematic to be suggested in words (343).

Agee could have clarified this concept if he had defined, instead of

only suggesting, the fundamental difference between the novel and the

film: Language is as basic to the novel as photography is to the

film. For this reason, certain subjects which inherently contain a

great deal of movement, like anarchic satire, are more suited to the

dynamic, visual medium of cinema.

More recent film theorists have also expressed the conviction

that the film and the novel are distinct aesthetic forms, each shaping

and affecting material in its own way. Agee would accept Suzanne

Langer's comparison of film with dream in the mode of presentation.

In creating a virtual present with direct apparition, the film is not

a new technique; it is a new poetic mode. "This is not the mode of

fiction, which is 'like' memory, or of drama, which is 'like' action.

It is the mode of dream, with the dreamer always at the center of

it."[33] Ingmar Bergman distinguishes distinct forms, but less

convincingly than Langer. He believes that the novel works primarily

through print to the intellect and the will, while the film works

through pictures directly to feelings.[34] This statement is ironic

in that most films of Bergman, like those of Bunuel and Antonioni,

are more static and intellectual than the more visual, emotional

films of Kurosawa and Fellini.

George Bluestone argues that ballet, an art in time and motion,

is as comparable to the static art of architecture as the film, also

a time art, is to the static novel.[35] Interested in establishing

the fact of two separate forms, Bluestone does not argue for the

superiority of one form over another. The primary principle that

[33] "A Note on the Film," in Film: A Montage of Theories, ed. Richard Dyer Mac Cann (New York, 1966), p. 199.

[34] Four Screenplays of Ingmar Bergman, trans. Lars Malrustrom and David Kushner (New York, 1960), p. xviii.

[35] Novels into Films (Berkeley, 1966), p. 5.

follows from this distinction is that a film should not be assessed
on the basis of its fidelity to the novel from which it was adapted.
Reviewing David Lean's treatment of Great Expectations, Agee states
that it seems unimportant how well or ill somebody else's classic
is brought to the screen (289). Each work must be judged
independently. Of the treatment of Hemingway's To Have and Have Not,
he writes that the film has so little to do with the novel, "I can
see no point in discussing its faithfulness." He then reviews it
favorably, saying it is one of the best movies in some time (121).
This principle of two different forms, even in the case of
adaptations, is ignored or dismissed by the majority of movie-goers,
as well as by some critics. Stanley Kauffmann still persists in
judging a film in terms of the work from which it was adapted: his
partial rejection of Rosemary's Baby is based on his own interpretation
of Ira Levin's novel, which happens to be different from the
interpretation by director Roman Polanski.[36]

Agee believes that the film for too long has been print-
dominated and over-adapted. Concerning Aldous Huxley's screenplay
of his story Giocando Smile, he writes, "a rather literary movie,
but most movies aren't even that; much less are they real movies"
(294). His scale of values is enunciated: a "cinematic" movie is
preferable to a "literary" movie. The major weakness in the film
version of For Whom the Bell Tolls is that the characters talk too
much. There is a valiant effort to keep Hemingway's characters
intact, but to no avail since the adaptation is too literary, too

theatrical.[37] Somerset Maugham's The Moon and Sixpence suffered a worse fate, since it is probably the most faithful treatment any novel has ever received. This "faithfulness" produces "a still life more than a moving picture." The device of flashbacks by two narrators works out well in print but proves disastrous on the screen, especially since the adapter-director Albert Lewin has the novel read almost word by word. As a result, this film's action is frozen "into little more than a set of magic-lantern slides."[38]

Because the novel and film represent distinct modes, adaptations seldom make excellent cinema. The very prestige and literary glamour of a successful novel sometimes can inhibit the adapter and shrivel up his plastic imagination. As George Bluestone aptly puts it, "the film-maker, like Lot's wife, is frequently immobilized in the very act of looking over his shoulder."[39] Michelangelo Antonioni declared recently that he never again will adapt a novel into a film, since he prefers to work on original scripts.[40] The reason for this opposition to adaptations seems obvious: the film is a visual medium while the novel is a printed medium.

Word dominated films, whether adaptations or original scripts,

---

[37] "For Whom the Bell Tolls," Time, XLII (August 2, 1943), 55-60.

[38] "The Moon and Sixpence," Time, XL (September 19, 1942), 96-98.

[39] Bluestone, p. 218.

[40] "Antonioni," a Channel 13 N.E.T. television program, conducted by Stanley Kauffmann (March 5, 1967, 9:00 - 10:30 P.M. in New York).

constitute an inferior form of cinema (40). Ingrained tradition of
the word affected even Second World War documentaries, which were
marvelous opportunities for pure visual cinema. Agee denounces,
without reservation, word-oriented films.

> The normal native commentary, well measuring our
> loss of cinematic instinct, heckles and humiliates
> the screen image, and pounds it, like the nagging
> of a shrew, a salesman, a preacher, a demagogue, a
> pimp, or all five combined; we use films to
> illustrate the rotten words we worship (34).

According to film-maker Maya Deren, influence of the word has been
the primary deterrent to the development of an independent cinematic
idiom. The narrative sequence has been so customary that we have
thought in terms of the continuity-logic of the literary narrative
instead of the discontinuous, simultaneous flow of visual images,
the language of film. "Once we arrive at an independent cinematic
idiom, the present subservience of cinema to the literary story will
appear unbelievably primitive."[41] The trend in the 1960's seems to be
in the direction desired by Agee, Deren, and others. The young
directors now dominating the film festivals, like the 1966 Film
Festival in Lincoln Center, are asserting their freedom from bondage
to literature. No longer do they follow the rules of the novel or
stage play. Their rich visual vocabularies declare, as the _Time_
reviewer self-consciously rhymes, that they mean "to write with their
lens and not with their pens."[42]

The popular belief has been that the film can not rival the

---

[41]
"Cinema As An Art Form," in Introduction to the Art of the Movies,
ed. Lewis Jacobs (New York, 1960), pp. 260-261.

[42]
"The Eyes Have It," _Time_, (September 23, 1966), p. 74.

novel's depths. Penelope Gilliatt refers in a recent review to the
cinema's incompatibility with sustained ideas, as though the point is
axiomatic.[43] One of the pioneering masters of the film documentary,
Robert Flaherty, accepted the film's subservient position in this
regard. The film, he wrote, can not convey what the printed word can,
but what it can say, it does with more conviction.[44] And Walter Kerr
states that indisputably words are subtler than pictures because they
can cut to the heart's core. An imaginary contest between the finest
film ever made and the finest play ever written "must inevitably end
in victory for the play, by virtue of its verbal profundity."[45] Even
media-oriented Marshall McLuhan suggests that the film can not rival
the word in "depth symbolism."[46]

In a radical stance for the 1940's, Agee advanced the argument
that the film is capable of plumbing the most profound depths of the
human condition because it is not hampered by the medium of words.
William Wellman's G.I. Joe is cited as portraying silently and
uninsistently the change in the face of the youngest of the soldiers
after his first battle, "from that of a lonely, brave, frightened boy
to something shriveled and poisoned beyond suggesting by words" (173).
Essentially the same concept is offered in Agee's essay "Comedy's
Greatest Era," an analysis of the silent screen comedians from Keaton

---

[43] "On and Off Target," The New Yorker (September 7, 1968), pp. 85-88.

[44] Edward Fischer, The Screen Arts (New York, 1960), p. 95.

[45] How Not to Write a Play (Milwaukee, 1954), p. 224.

[46] McLuhan, p. 288.

to Chaplin. The more gifted of these men learned, by visual means
alone, to communicate complex emotional states more eloquently than
most language has ever managed to, and they "discovered beauties of
comic motion which are hopelessly beyond reach of words" (3). Agee
offers the climax of Chaplin's City Lights as evidence.

> At the end of City Lights the blind girl who has
> regained her sight, thanks to the tramp, sees him
> for the first time. She has imagined and antici-
> pated him as princely, to say the least; and it
> has never seriously occurred to him that he is
> inadequate. She recognizes who he must be by his
> shy, confident, shining joy as he comes silently
> toward her. And he recognizes himself, for the
> first time, through the terrible changes in her
> face. The camera just exchanges a few quiet
> close-ups of the emotions which shift and
> intensify in each face. It is enough to shrivel
> the heart to see (10).

For these reasons, Agee believes that the deepest emotion, and the
richest, most poignant poetry are in Chaplin's silent films.

As a film critic, Agee is interested in comparing and contrasting
the film with the other arts, not in submitting claims of superiority.
I feel certain he would object to Eisenstein's tendency toward
pompous, blanket generalizations: "Only the film-element commands a
means for an adequate presentation of the whole course of thought
through a disturbed mind."[47] In reviewing Huston's "San Pietro," Agee
states that close to the essence of the power of the film is its
ability to present pictures, free from urging or comment, and so
ordered that they are radiant with "illimitable suggestions of meaning

---
[47] Eisenstein, p. 104. cf. Agee's Time review of "Farewell My Lovely"
(December 18, 1944), which sets forth his belief in the medium's
ability to capture the whole course of thought, as well as several
states of mind.

and mystery" (164). Thus, neither extravagant claims nor defeatist admissions mark Agee's contrasting and comparing the film to the novel. In believing the film capable of expressing depths as well as the novel, he anticipated a more recent development, an interplay between the two separate forms. The films of Bergman, Antonioni, Resnais and Godard are representative of the way contemporary films reveal multiple meanings, symbolism in depth, evocative atmospheres, enigmatic characters. Today the film has stepped into what used to be considered by many theorists, not Agee, the sole province of the novel.[48]

As with the novel, Agee insists on maintaining distinct aesthetic criteria for judging the film and the stage play. He sees the essential differences between these forms as a greater directness and intimacy in the theater and a more visual orientation in the film. An Olsen and Johnson stage success fails as a film because their "ability to exude a kind of ectoplasm which engulfs a theater audience and makes it participate in the show is necessarily cut off when the show is confined to the screen" (335). Besides this type of engulfing directness, the theater has another dimension which distinguishes it from the film. Saroyan's The Time of Your Life has a cabaret-type of dependency on flesh-and-blood intimacy with a live audience. The film adapted from the play, however, does not contain this intimacy, and hence becomes dull and slack (387). Agee believes that good stage technique does its work through the ears, whereas good film technique does its work through the eyes. He would be inclined

---

Hollis Alpert, The Dreams and the Dreamers (New York, 1962), p. 245.

to accept René Clair's dictum: "a blind man in a regular theater and a deaf mute in a movie theater should still get the essentials from the performance." [49]

In general, Agee opposes adaptations which are little more than filmed stage performances. As "literary" films tend to be inferior cinema, so do "theatrical" films. Yet, he acknowledges exceptions. The value in permanently recording a superb stage performance like Paul Lukas' in Watch on the Rhine, [50] and the possibility of assembling an exceptional cast to portray a noted work are recognized. With the 1946 version of Shaw's Caesar and Cleopatra, the audience could focus on the actors' every action by virtue of the camera, and hear every inflection by virtue of the microphone, so that, in this instance the dialogue was spoken intelligibly, and Shaw's insights were understood and lucidly conveyed (213).

Pauline Kael has followed Agee's lead in adopting a moderate position toward film adaptations of stage plays. [51] The camera can intensify our consciousness of the human face, pick up details, and

---

[49]
    Hans Richter, "The Film as an Original Art Form," in Introduction to the Art of the Movies, ed. Lewis Jacobs (New York, 1960), p. 286.

[50]
    "Watch on the Rhine," Time, XLII (September 6, 1943), 94-96. Because of this critical tenet, Agee would accept the current practice of filming actual stage productions such as Burton's Hamlet and Olivier's Othello, even though most film critics have thoroughly rejected them.

[51]
    Joseph McBride, "Mr. Macdonald, Mr. Kauffmann and Miss Kael," Film Heritage, II (Summer 1967), 26-34. In Mr. McBride's estimation, Miss Kael is "the best American film critic now practicing." With the masses, however, she has not fared as well. McCalls severed their relationship after Miss Kael mercilessly assaulted The Sound of Music. Since January, 1968, she has been writing brilliant reviews for the New Yorker.

direct our eye toward subtleties of the performance. She cites

the film version of Strindberg's <u>Miss Julie</u> as an example of an

adaptation which treats the stage and screen as if they were

"opposed media." Director Alf Sjoberg subjects the play to a

"chemical change."[52]   Although considered as distinct media, the

stage and screen have never been treated as opposites in Kael's

criticism. Hollis Alpert, on the other hand, has declared that

there is no essential difference between stage and screen. They

both are concerned ultimately with human drama, and only the

theorists have separated the two media. Since the human drama is

the nucleus of both media in Agee's criticism, he would be inclined

to sympathize with this viewpoint. Yet, because he believes that

motion and a visual quality are vital to film, and not to theater,

he would ultimately reject Alpert's position.

In one review Agee refers to the commonplace observation that

movie and musical form are closely related (241). He could have

cited such film masters as Sergei Eisenstein, who compares the film

to music in terms of rhythm, overtones, and undertones. The more

recent film-makers, who attained prominence after Agee's lifetime,

have continued to compare the two forms. Alain Resnais, for one,

believes that the dialogue in <u>Hiroshima Mon Amour</u> is more important

as music than as simple dialogue. Musical structure to Resnais is

---

52

"Movies, the Desperate Art," in <u>Films: An Anthology</u>, ed.
Dan Talbot (New York, 1959), p. 196.

vital to cinema.[53] Ingmar Bergman declares that film is most like
music in that it tends to be more emotional than intellectual; also,
rhythm is pronounced in both forms.[54] Ernest Lindgren points out
that there has always been a close relationship between music and
film because the latter is above all an art of movement.[55]

Agee defines the relationship between film and music as one of
mood, tempo, rhythm, and timing. In attacking the charge of
repetitiousness leveled upon Farrebique, he agrees that the film is
indeed repetitious, "exactly in the sense that the imitation and
counterpoint and recurrence in a Mozart symphony are repetitious,
and somewhere near as satisfying" (298). Timing is of the essence
in both forms. Bosley Crowther rejects Carl Dreyer's Day of Wrath
on the ground that it is so slow it imposes on the average person's
time, and that it is made only for "cultists." Agee replies,
more trenchantly than usual, that he feels certain Mr. Crowther,
upon hearing the slow movement of Beethoven's "Archduke Trio," would
find "the tax of Beethoven's slow and ponderous tempo upon the
average person's time -- meaning, one supposes, his time -- an

---

[53] "'Hiroshima Mon Amour,' a Composite Interview with Alain Resnais,"
in Film: Book 2, Films of Peace and War, ed. Robert Hughes (New York,
1962), p. 56. It seems that Resnais is emphasizing the close relationship between the two forms by means of an exaggerated statement.
His dialogue, in terms of verbal meanings, is essential to characterization, development of the theme, and the symbolism in Hiroshima
Mon Amour, and thus is more important than his statement suggests.

[54] Bergman, xvii.

[55] Lindgren, p. 137.

equally presumptuous imposition" (303). Agee concludes his defense
of the film by contending that slowness can be used as artfully as
speed in either music or in film. Agee's first argument seems
unconvincing. Repetitiousness is not as satisfying in cinema as in
music. Films need a continued progression, more so than pieces of
music. There is no cinematic equivalent to the first movement of
Beethoven's Fifth Symphony, a masterpiece of musical repetition.
Agee's second argument is more solid: films have to move, but they
can do so slowly, as Antonioni's work has demonstrated.

In addition to a similarity, there can exist, in the hands of a
talented director, an inter-play between film and painting. Olivier's
French court in Henry V is reminiscent of a pre-Renaissance painting
in its "fragility, elegance, spaciousness, and color." Olivier also
keeps the photographic perspective as shallow as possible, as they are
in medieval paintings (363). Some film-makers have intentionally
injected art references into their films. Pudovkin, in reference to
Mother, tells of the inspiration he received from various paintings:
Velasquez' "Bollo," which brought the famous camera angle of the
monumental policeman into being; Van Gogh's "Prison Courtyard;" the
haggard blue-period paintings of Picasso; Rouault's "Three Judges;" and
others.[56]

Agee tends to reject the "artiness" of this practice. The
enriching relationship and influence which is possible between
painting and film can easily become cloyed by a director's

---

[56] George Huaco, The Sociology of Film Art (New York, 1965), p. 112.

self-consciousness or self-indulgence. In reviewing Carl Dreyer's
Day of Wrath, Agee writes that he ordinarily cares little for
approximations or reproductions of famous paintings achieved by a
director's artful composing, as Dreyer did with Rembrandt. Dreyer
nevertheless managed to do this so uninsistently that the picture
remains clear of "culturalism" (304). For the film-maker who can
avoid the temptations toward compositional pretensions, there is
great potential in integrating and synthesizing various art forms
into the film medium. Agee never mentions his feelings toward the
obvious, recurrent use of reproductions of famous scenes in The Birth
of a Nation. By the use of stills, Griffith informs audiences that
these scenes, like Ford's theater on the night of Lincoln's
assassination and Lee's surrender to Grant at Appomatox, are "after"
well-known paintings of the events. The film's over-all force and
flow, as well as the historical context in which these scenes are
placed, insure against any form of static, pseudo-artistic posturing.

Sergei Eisenstein, fully immersed by training in all of the fine
arts, consciously strove to parallel the compositional elements of
individual shots in Alexander Nevsky with its musical lines. He
believes that the essence of film is "organic synthesis," and that,
above all, the film is a genuinely synthetic art.[57] Agee in this
vein calls attention to the creative possibilities deriving from
synthesis and integration.

---

[57] Eisenstein, p. 193.

> But Olivier's films set up an equilateral triangle
> between the screen, the stage, and literature. And
> between the screen, the stage, and literature they
> establish an interplay, a shimmering splendor, of
> the disciplined vitality which is art (396).

Olivier framed the incomparable poetry and theatrical inventiveness
of Shakespeare in visually alive films, thus drawing upon the
strengths of three media.

The film reviews, like this one, so frequently and freely touch
upon the other arts that Manny Farber believes Agee was motivated by
a desire to bridge Hollywood with the highest mounts of art and
"had a dozen ways to move films into the museum."[58] John Simon
attempted recently to determine why Agee was such an "exceptional
film critic." Besides his humanity, sensitivity, and literary gifts,
Agee is credited with a "multiplicity of interests." He was so good
a film critic because he was not <u>only</u> a film critic.[59] Simon's
observation is valid, but he could have specified Agee's informed
appreciation of Beethoven, Gluck, Mozart, and Picasso.

In the past two decades, there have been an increasing number of
disputes over the precise nature of the film. Dr. Siegfried Kracauer
argues that each medium has a specific nature which "invites certain
kinds of communications while obstructing others."[60] Because the

---

[58] "Star-Gazing for the Middlebrows," New Leader, XLI (December 5, 1958), 14-15.

[59] "James Agee," Film Heritage, III (Fall 1967), 35.

[60] Theory of Film (New York, 1965), p. 3.

film has evolved from photography, it is drawn to external, physical reality; its affinity is toward the physical world, the surface of things. As such, the film is not amenable to the more subjective, private states, nor to tragedy; it cannot penetrate to the core of life, and therefore intellectual or ideological topics are not suitable. Kracauer's thesis is now dominant in much of film criticism.

This topic has been debated since the inception of the film. The two French pioneers saw fundamentally divergent tendencies in the new moving pictures. Lumière, like Kracauer, believed the camera should be used to record the physical world around him. His filming of a moving train caused a sensation. On the other hand, Méliès, the fabulist, envisioned a breathtaking range of fanciful possibilities in the medium, like a trip to the moon.

Historically, a score of film-makers and theorists have been of this latter Méliès, anti-Kracauer school. V. I. Pudovkin taught that every object on the screen should have not photographic, but cinematographic essence. The director's task is not to record what is in front of his camera, but to arrange it.[61] Richard Winnington charges the mature film-maker with the responsibility of seeing his material as something far richer than the actual, as indeed something removed from the literal: "the paradox of the cinema is that it is anything but photographic."[62]

[61]
    Film Technique and Film Acting (New York, 1960), p. 25.

[62]
    Drawn and Quartered (London, 1948, now out of print) as quoted in Paul Rotha, Rotha on the Film (Fair Lawn, 1958), p. 32.

Carl Dreyer, identified with realism, calls unexpectedly for more
abstraction in films, particularly through the use of color and other
new techniques. The capacity to abstract is essential to all artistic
creation.

> We have got stuck with photography. Photography
> as a means of reporting, of sightseeing, has
> compelled the film to remain with its feet on
> the ground. We have to wrench the film out of
> the embrace of naturalism. We have to tell
> ourselves it is a waste of time to copy reality.
> We must use the camera to create a new language
> of style, a new artistic form.[63]

The film artist must, Dreyer believes, explore inner, not outer life.
Ralph Stephenson and J. R. Debrix, in a recent statement, logically
maintain that the Kracauer thesis is an argument reductio ad
absurdum. Advocates of cinema total, drawn by the compulsive realism
of photography, consider the film imperfect to the extent that it
falls short of complete reality. In this view, the ideal cinema
would capture total reality. But, the authors point out, "if this
dream were realized, then the cinema would be reality -- and would
cease to be art."[64]

Agee's solution is to fuse the abstract with the realistic.
His respect for the power of the film to capture unstaged reality, by
means of photographic realism, is steady.

---

[63] "Thoughts on My Craft" in Film: A Montage of Theories, ed.
Richard Dyer Mac Cann, p. 313. I suspect that Dreyer expresses these
thoughts, written in 1955, more out of a sense of confinement or
chagrin than conviction, since he has continued to maintain a strict
level of photographic realism in Ordet (1955) and Gertrud (1964).

[64] The Cinema as Art (Baltimore, 1965), p. 33.

Yet, his call for something beyond the actual, the poetry which resides in every real object, is equally insistent. He would reject Kracauer's thesis that the camera's sole function is to record physical reality, on the grounds that a film must have more than just striking photography. In a review of a film concerning horses, Agee writes, "Whenever the horses are busy, it is pleasant to look at; but so are moving clouds, or water, without too much credit to their recorder" (149).

An historical illustration of Agee's position is G. W. Pabst's films of New Realism. Both in The Joyless Street and The Love of Jeanne Ney, made in Germany during the late 1920's, Pabst composed real-life material with veracity as his fundamental objective. He did not design pictorial compositions; his work is not picturesque, it is photographic. He attempted to make the spectator feel "how true," rather than "how beautiful." Agee would endorse both the rejection of artiness and the search for significance in Pabst's work. Further, he would dismiss Kracauer's belief that the film can neither penetrate the inner life nor handle intellectual topics. Arguing for at least the equality of the film with the novel's ability to embody complexity and subtlety, Agee is clear in his documentation.

In treating themes, subjects, and materials in the film, Agee opts for the universal and the original. John Huston's The Treasure of the Sierra Madre approaches global appeal because it reaches the least and most sophisticated members of an audience. Nearly all of the best films have this quality in common; Hollywood, regretably, has tended to embrace the artificial. Agee points out this

self-defeating trend in I'll Be Seeing You, which has a "simple"
boy-meets-girl story. After studio processing, the boy turns out to
be a soldier on psychiatric leave, and the girl turns out to be an
inmate on prison leave. Coincidentally, it is Christmas, which in
this film is presented as the most mawkish time of the year.[65]
Hollywood's genius for the artificial has not disappeared since Agee's
time. In the United States in 1968, while riots and racial hatreds
plague the cities, and the country seethes with discontent at the war
in Vietnam, Hollywood has offered, respectively, a whitewashed Sidney
Poitier in Guess Who's Coming to Dinner? and another John Wayne
glorification of war, The Green Berets.

Universal themes spring from specific, even local concerns and
portrayals. Agee believes that "intimate specification" is less
dispensable to valid art than generalization; most of the best films,
in fact, "are and would always have to be developed locally, and
primarily for local audiences" (181). Though too parochial in outlook,
this statement signifies Agee's attempt to elucidate the principle
that the deeper the artist plumbs the specific, the wider is likely
to be the application of his meaning. An embodiment of this principle
can be found in Satyajit Ray's works, undertaken after the period of
Agee's reviews. Able in practice to convey to his audience the whole
world by focusing on Bengal, the Indian director has theorized that
it is from the specific that the universal emerges. A feeling of
closeness to all mankind permeates the Apu trilogy and Ray's other

---

[65] "The New Pictures," Time, XLV (January 22, 1945), 91-92.

films, because he has been true to one corner of the world.[66]

In theory, Agee most admires original or new work undertaken for the film. His main reservation with Olivier's Henry V concerns its being re-worked material. Without the aid or hindrance of a classic, it would be even more commendable (236). In 1947 Agee applauded David Lean's Great Expectations, but dissented from a rather sizable faction at that time which considered it the apex of achievement for the medium. Only "a transfiguration rather than a translation" would deserve such praise. There are enormous difficulties in creating new material for the screen. Agee wrote that in seeing the 1947 Wake Island, the first American film on the war made after armistice, he was prepared for the worst, because only people of exceptional talent have even a chance of not being paralyzed, for a considerable time, by a new subject (243). Unfortunately, as well as disappointingly, Agee as a film writer in Hollywood, with several practical creative opportunities, wrote only one original script (the never-produced Noa-Noa on the life of Gauguin), while the other four published scripts were adaptations. He must have discovered that it is easy in theory to demand, but difficult in practice to produce, original scripts. Only the most distinguished among contemporary directors have been able to work repeatedly on original scripts: Bergman, Fellini, Antonioni, Godard.

The preference for a basically simple story is consistent with the rest of Agee's aesthetic outlook. Great and simple are adjectives

66
Erik Barnouw and S. Krishnaswamy, Indian Film (New York, 1963), p. 235.

often joined in recognition of certain films: The Bicycle Thief,

Farrebique, Man's Hope. The Bicycle Thief, concerning a father and

son's heartbreaking search for a stolen bicycle, which is their means

of livelihood, represents a type of fiction which few writers seem

able to attempt, or even respect (229). Brief Encounter has a

"simple and important" theme, the uneventful affair of two decent,

middle-aged married persons, of the type too often neglected in the

film medium (215). Madame Curie is appreciated for focusing on a

matter seldom attempted on the screen: the beauty, dignity, and calm

of a marriage earnestly, not romantically, undertaken.[67] Other basic,

simple subjects worthy of film treatment are the depiction of "the

daily and lifelong effort of rural man as a part of nature and as a

portion of eternity,"[68] and the bringing up of a child, which Agee

terms one of the few dramatic subjects in the movies, at that time,

worthy of a second thought (70). He poetically realized this

opportunity through the autobiographical character of Rufus in A Death

in the Family.

Critics have divided over the desirability of simple plots.

Edward Fischer states that of two dramas, one of a man's heart breaking

over a freckle-faced girl, and another heart breaking over desire to

win a kingdom, the former tells the audience more about life, since it

occurs with greater frequency and is within the audience's frame of

---

[67] "Ideal Woman", Time, XLII (December 20, 1943), 154-58.

[68] "Farrebique," Time, LI (March 15, 1948), 100-104.

reference. Of course, this is only an aesthetic platitude without
an examination of the artist's treatment of the story.[69] Fischer,
however, is speaking in general terms of the suitability of plot
structures for the screen. He believes that The Bicycle Thief showed
the audience that the loss of a bicycle can cause as much suffering
as the loss of an empire.[70] Richard Schickel, film critic for Life,
writes, contrary to Fischer and Agee, that one of the reasons for
the decline of neo-realism was the too ordinary, uninspiring stories,
as in The Bicycle Thief. Such a film only makes partial use of the
medium's potential, and it forces attention on "people who may be
tragic, but who are basically rather uninteresting as fictional
subjects because of their limited experiences, intelligences, and
sensibilities."[71] It seems rather strange to say that a character can
be so portrayed as to be tragic, and yet be "uninteresting." To be
sure, The Bicycle Thief and other films about ordinary people, like
Brief Encounter, have gained in stature from the test of time.

Fischer further maintains that in order for subjects to be
suitable for the film, they must need the medium in the sense of

[69] I. A. Richards, Principles of Literary Criticism (New York 1925),
p. 187, in interpreting Tolstoy's "infection theory", makes an
important point. A story can be as peculiar as possible, as long as
common interests are aroused.

[70] Edward Fischer, p. 74.

[71] Movies, The History of an Art and an Institution (New York, 1964),
p. 144.

72
demanding to be both visual and in motion. As fundamentally
important as motion and the visual are in Agee's criticism, he never
asks whether a film moves or is visual. Rather, he asks what does it
mean; what significance does it contain? Does the idea have
universal appeal; is it a new or original treatment; does it have a
basically simple framework; is it concerned with moral or human
problems? These constitute Agee's criteria for worthy filmic
concepts and materials.

Given valid, mature ideas and materials to work with, what
chances existed for their properly being expressed during the 1940's?
Throughout his tenure as critic, Agee faced this practical question,
since it represents the making, distributing, and showing of films.
Although he praised the communicative nature and potentialities of
the medium, he was,at the same time, acutely aware of the medium's
limitations. "Hollywood," in its broadest context, not only in its
denotation as a geographical location, represented the severest
handicap.

The basic problem was too much money ill spent. Affluence can
be stifling when indiscriminately applied to artistic endeavors. In
one of his annual appraisals, Agee wished that the production team of
Val Lewton and Robert Wise be given no more than their usual

72
    Fischer, p. 114. This tenet is a popular one in contemporary film
theory. It is included in most syllabi for college film courses,
perhaps partly because of Fischer's well-known course at the
University of Notre Dame.

allotment of money, [73] since "a small budget has on the whole

sharpened their resourcefulness" (129). He stated more explicitly in

the review of Open City that his deepest hope for the future of films

was in their being made simply, with relatively little money (236).

Though certain artistic advantages obtain in having large operating

budgets, such as being able to secure a uniformly excellent cast

(Henry V), the net results are more often negative. Henry Miller in

1939 succinctly formulated the theory that "the more money a film

costs the worse it is apt to be." [74] Only a handful of directors

(David Lean with The Bridge on the River Kwai and, more recently,

Stanley Kubrick with 2001: A Space Odyssey) have surmounted this

obstacle successfully.

The father of the British documentary, John Grierson, years ago [75]

stated that there is nothing "quite as diffident as a million dollars."

Director Fred Zinnemann, successful commercially and artistically with

such work as High Noon and A Man for All Seasons, wrote that rarely

---

[73]
Agee's wish has not come true: Robert Wise, in the 1960's, directed two multi-million dollar productions, The Sound of Music and The Sand Pebbles, both less than critical successes, though The Sound of Music has deservedly enjoyed popular acclaim and is one of the biggest money-makers in Hollywood history.

[74]
Manny Farber, "Underground Films," in Film: An Anthology, ed. Daniel Talbot (New York, 1959), p. 376.

[75]
Ernest Lindgren, The Art of the Film (New York, 1963), p. 28.

is a man of vision in charge of a great industrial enterprise like a
Hollywood studio. Even more rarely would this type of magnate risk
experimenting with several millions of dollars.[76]   A concrete example
of this occurred during the filming of Huston's The Treasure of The
Sierra Madre. Jack Warner, not seeing rushes of singing, dancing,
and cucaracha-type color sent back to the studio from the location-
shooting in Mexico, threatened to call off production.[77]

Such facts of Hollywood life have had far-reaching effects on
the production of films. In no other art is the artist so completely
dependent on high finance. A man who is determined to succeed as a
writer can buy his paper for a few cents; his only other requirement,
as Anthony Trollope put it, is a piece of cobbler's wax to keep him
fastened in his chair. But even the most talented individual has
little chance of making a film for commercial distribution unless he
can command large capital resources.[78]   These very impositions and
restrictions on film makers gave impetus to the New Wave in France,
whose outstanding director and spokesman, Francois Truffaut,

------

[76]
Joanne Stang, "Tis the Season to Be Zinnemann," The New York
Times, March 5, 1967, D13.

[77]
Ezra Goodman, The Fifty Year Decline and Fall of Hollywood (New
York, 1962), p. 179. Since Agee's time, the tyrannical days of Cohn
and Mayer have vanished, the character of the studios has altered, and
other improvements have taken place. Yet it would be fanciful to
claim that Agee's demands have been satisfied by current Hollywood
practices. In a recent Time cover story on the cinema (December 8,
1967, p. 73), Stefan Kanfer wrote that "the old dinosaurs in the
corner offices have finally given way to younger dinosaurs."

[78]
Lindgren, p. 28. The inexpensive Super 8 mm cameras have produced
a rash of student and amateur "movies," but these are not marketable,
commercial products.

declared independence from the film industry: he would have no extras,
no expensive sets, no astronomical budgets. Yet even a gifted Truffaut
was not immune to commercial suffocation. With Hollywood's financial
undergirding, he directed recently an adaptation of the best seller
Fahrenheit 451, employing the practices he once condemned: a star-
studded cast of thousands, expensive location-shooting, an enormous
budget. The New Wave, after defections like this, seems to have spent
its force. One would like to accept Edward Wagenknecht's challenge
that every artist through history has had to overcome the limitations
inherent in his medium, and if he fails in this he fails as an artist.
He rejects as myth "the Drama of the Endless Struggle between the
Artist and the Harsh, Conscienceless, Commerical Monster known as
Hollywood" and gallantly quotes from Goethe, "In der Beschrankung
zeigt sich erst der Meister."[79]

Agee would reject this as a simplification. A Henry Moore
overcoming the limitations inherent in bronze is qualitatively different from a young artist overcoming the stranglehold which Hollywood
has had on the production and distribution of films. For these
reasons, Agee viewed Hollywood as inimical to art. He over-stated the
case against Hollywood after seeing particularly offensive movies.
At these times, he saw a world of compromise, made up of racketeers,
all looking after their own special interests. He charged that few
Americans either behind or in front of cameras gave any evidence of
respecting either themselves or others as human beings. On both ends
of the camera only a depressingly few people were not essentially

---

[79] The Movies in the Age of Innocence (Oklahoma, 1962), pp. 214-215.

"promoters, little racketeers, interested in 'the angle'" (224). Even
after allowing for the exaggeration in Agee's evangelical zeal to re-
form Hollywood, we should entertain little doubt that the finest
Hollywood products were in some ways compromised (e.g., the studio
music in Minelli's The Clock). "Lucrative exploitation," instead of
artistic integrity, was too often the objective of the "promoters".
To Each His Own, which could have been a searing analysis of a social
problem, is gross exploitation of audiences for commercial gain.

> From the moment the girl knows she is illicitly
> pregnant she acts like the moral coward nearly
> everyone in Hollywood and in the audience requires
> her to be, and that every plot complication and
> tearjerk from there on proceeds from, and exploits,
> premises of cowardice, cynicism, and the rottenest
> kinds of sentimentality (225).

Ezra Goodman, who for the past twenty-five years has worked in
Hollywood, has issued a more recent, if over-stated, condemnation.
"In the Hollywood studios, the mass attack of a mob of half-wits in
sport shirts and fifty-dollar shoes stamps any real idea to death
before it leaves the studio." [80] At present, a script for a major
picture might go through, in assembly-line fashion, as many as a
dozen rewrites by a dozen different writers. One picture completed
in 1967, This Property Is Condemned, employed the services of sixteen
writers. It has also been accepted Hollywood policy that a writer
hammers out a script on his own, and then moves on to another job.
Relatively few script writers work closely with the director or make

[80] Goodman, p. 159. Although Goodman, as a critic, habitually
mistakes peevishness for humor, he does speak with more authority in
this instance.

revisions as work progresses on the set.[81] For many palpable reasons, Agee, in the 1940's, viewed Hollywood as detrimental to art. Unfortunately, some of these conditions exist twenty-five years later.

Even dealing with the much-maligned Hollywood, Agee discerned a world of grays, not black and whites. At times, in his impetuous manner, he excessively condemned Hollywood. Yet, at other times, he stated that Hollywood should not be made the scapegoat for all that was unfortunate about the movies. In discussing Cinema 16, a non-commercial film society, he outlined the particular temptations which accrue to such non-Hollywood ventures, pointing out that pure, artistic motives can not guarantee a good film (308). He also acknowledged that Hollywood produced most of the "good popular art" in the world. The vacuous British productions of the late 1930's and early 1940's, like Rembrandt and Things to Come, which were patterned after some Hollywood successes of the period, vividly illustrated that no country could "out-Hollywood Hollywood" in terms of flair, exuberance, and showmanship.[82]

Agee further realized that in the late 1940's Hollywood was truly at the crossroads. There is a reference in the review of Wilson to "a Hollywood scared to death of mature responsibilities yet eager to assume them, and willing now and again to bet its shirt on

---

[81] Peter Bart, "Doesn't Anyone Love a Writer?" The New York Times (March 6, 1966), XII. Agee as script writer worked closely with Huston on The African Queen, making changes as filming progressed.

[82] Arthur Knight, The Liveliest Art (New York, 1957), p. 208.

the attempt."[83]   He detected some promising signs that Hollywood was
entering puberty, but, the Motion Picture Production Code, strong at
that time, was a discouraging factor.[84]

The Code, in fact, was the strongest force for retardation of
the film during Agee's period of reviewing. Not imposed from the
outside, it arose from and reflected the very ills plaguing Hollywood:
immature fantasy and hypocrisy. It only deepened the vices for which
it originally was created. The Code, in totally prohibiting certain
subjects, distorted reality. What made the Code-produced brand of
reality credible to audiences was the technical skill of Hollywood.
Realistic styles of acting, location-shooting, and almost limitless
resources to reproduce reality could make an average screenplay of
half-truths convey an impression of life.[85]   Olga Martin, secretary to
Joseph I. Breen, former Director of the Production Code Administration,
proclaimed the Code philosophy: "The American audience in particular
demands a 'cheerful ending' in answer to a deeply-felt human need for
a kindly philosophy of life -- the kind of homespun philosophy

---

[83]
"Wilson," Time, XLIV (August 7, 1944), 84-86.

[84]
In the late 1960's, Hollywood is focusing on shocking themes in a
manner unthinkable ten years ago. Although a clumsy, soggy affair,
Mark Ryder's film version of D. H. Lawrence's The Fox, distributed
commercially on a large scale, treats lesbianism, even including a nude
scene of auto-eroticism. In this case, Hollywood is sensational but
not mature; with The Graduate and Bonnie and Clyde, Hollywood is
shocking and mature.

[85]
Schickel, p. 118.

exemplified by Will Rogers and Marie Dressler."[86]

In the 1950's the same type of official Puritanism still existed. The Moon is Blue was denied a Code seal of approval because of the words "virgin" and "seduce," and The Man with the Golden Arm was denied a seal because it concerned drug addiction, which, according to the Code, did not exist.[87] The Legion of Decency played a pivotal role in influencing these actions by the Production Code because of "C" ratings given to both films. In one of his reviews, Agee alluded to "the sinister forces of Decency." In general, he made little effort to disguise his disgust with the Legion of Decency, which proved to be a force for the repression of mature or serious treatments of controversial topics. Relevant to this concept, R. G. Collingwood has stated that bad art results not from expressing what is in itself evil, but "arises when instead of expressing these emotions we disown them, wishing to think ourselves innocent of the emotions that horrify us."[88] The Production Code and the Legion of Decency were two factors in the artlessness which plagued Hollywood because they, in effect, disowned seduction, drug addiction, and other "unfit" subjects.

Hypocrisy characterized Hollywood's continued observance of the Code. Claude Binyon, a director-writer, charged, with some

---

[86] Hollywood's Movie Commandments (New York, 1937), p. 53.

[87] Alpert, p. 219.

[88] The Principles of Art (New York, 1961), p. 284.

justification, that many movie-makers capitalized on censorship.
"Hollywood must never permit censorship to collapse -- it's far too
good for the box office."[89] This accusation touches upon the most
diseased parts of the Code, which has been described by George
Bluestone as the worst form of Victorianism in modern dress.[90] Agee
condemned the Code for what it engendered as well as for what it
prohibited.

> The Hays office became the Johnston Office. It
> remained possible, as before, to say almost
> anything if it was prurient, childish, or false
> enough in the first place and sneakily enough
> said in the second. It remained impossible, as
> before, to say anything whatever, without sneaking
> it, which might move or interest anyone past the
> moral age of five (238).

Restrictive provisions in any form obstruct the artist, whose desire
to practice his art can not be satisfied short of perfect liberty and
discipline (188).

The area of the Code most tightly restrictive, blatantly
hypocritical, seriously distorted, and frequently attacked was that
which dealt with human sexuality. The philosophy of the Code during
the 1940's was abundantly revealed in this bald statement: "The Code
considers passion as an unfit subject for screen presentation under
any circumstances."[91] Not only was passion unfit, but "adultery as a

[89]
  Goodman, p. 404.

[90]
  Bluestone, pp. 42-43.

[91]
  Martin, pp. 159-160.

subject should be avoided."[92] In other words, significant, vital areas of life simply did not exist in the world of the Code. Agee's response was satire and outright anger at these prohibitions. He wrote that Shirley Temple and John Agar as newlyweds in Fort Apache "handle the love interest as if they were sharing a soda-fountain special" (311). In reviewing The Unconquered, Agee noted the hypocrisy in Cecil B. DeMille's practice of getting away with all that the law would allow: "Miss Goddard, stripped down within an inch of the Johnston Office, is tethered for torture by the Indians and writhes exquisitely" (378). The Code, in effect, encouraged this type of intentional titillation, carried out within a framework of morality.[93]

At times, Agee directly bared such deceit. The story of Dr. Wassell depicts a heroic doctor during the war who helped Americans escape from Java.

> When the ship out of Java is strafed and a young
> woman is wounded, and her ankle is being bandaged,
> the occasion is used to slip in a discreet bit of
> leg art. . . . If a woman is wounded, her flesh may
> very possibly be exposed, but for heaven's sake
> photograph it in such a way that nobody in your
> audience can possibly gobble it up -- or vomit it
> out -- as criminally misplaced cheesecake (97).

In contrast to this degradation of sex was the French Children of Paradise, a mature handling of the subject. It honored its audience

---

92
   Martin, p. 277.

93
   For a scathing, convincing account of DeMille's hypocrisy, practiced over a period of decades, see Arthur Knight, The Liveliest Art, 113-116.

in assuming that it knew something about human reproduction, the
responsibilities inherent in sexual activity, and how explosively
dangerous certain situations could be. Such a mature treatment of a
fundamental part of life, which did not exist according to the Code,
made Agee"want to forage through Hollywood and various censors'
offices as a sort of improved, not to say dedicated, Jack the Ripper"
(247). During the 1940's he rightfully viewed and, more significantly,
exposed the Code as being as detrimental to the production and
distribution of films as the most lamentable practices of commercial
Hollywood.

Ambivalence marked Agee's attitude toward the Hollywood audience.
It was alternately condemned and praised, while being continually
reminded of its responsibilities. He understood the influence that
audiences can exert on an art form. As a negative force, the
Hollywood of the 1940's was characterized as immature, smug, and
content with "tinny romantic melodramas." On several occasions, his
enjoyment of a particular film was qualified by acknowledging, as if
morally bound to do so, that he probably would have yawned, not
laughed, at the same material on Broadway (64). He enjoyed watching
I Know Where I'm Going while, at the same time, realizing "how
shallow and shabby it would probably seem in print" (274). These
admissions indicate Agee's awareness not of any inherent weakness of
the medium, but of the relative immaturity of film audiences contrasted
with theatre audiences. Even more damaging to the medium was the
audience's tendency toward middle class smugness. The sugary
treatment of The Pearl was aimed at the big heart of the middle class,

which did not know anything about art, but liked what it knew (301). Such an audience militated against the emergence of the film as an art form. Rather, there was contentment with a series of Casablanca-type melodramas which have an artistic level of the now-fabled dime novel.

This type of stunted art had its defenders, who would have labeled Agee a "cultist." Olga Martin stated that very few screen patrons desired "sophisticated" pictures. "The critics who pretend to speak in their behalf overlook the fact that the demand for this type of drama emanates from a minority group far removed from the general movie public."[94] Not only latter-day Puritan upholders of righteousness defended the half-truths of Code-induced movies, but also a few serious film-makers, like Sir Carol Reed. Expressing dismay over the angry British films of the fifties, he argued that as long as the audience desires to have suspense and good actors in dramatic situations, with colorful and perhaps enchanting backgrounds, "why should we drag them to the cinema to look for an hour or two at a kitchen sink, a one-set film, the greasy dishes and the mental and moral miasma of certain elements in society?"[95] This type of attitude, which Agee abhorred, nourished the worst, most immature aspects of the film audience, which in turn served to retard the film's development.

---

[94] Martin, p. 51.

[95] Oakley, p. 228.

Unlike his attitude toward the Code, Agee detected some positive, though embryonic, stirrings in the film audience. This ambivalence is evident in his debate with Tolstoy's theory that the most reliable judge of art is a clean old peasant. Though it was never entirely convincing, Agee admitted that "it has strongly moved, interested, and unsettled me" (406). What unsettled him is a distrust of the soggy, sentimental bent of the masses, mixed with a conviction that art can flourish only in the midst of a diversified, robust audience. He saw this positive quality in film audiences, which resembled the crowds in Elizabethan theaters. "It is not likely that Shakespeare will ever again reach the lusty, semi-literate mass audience for which he wrote; today's equivalent fills the neighborhood movie houses" (396). Most good films draw much of their vitality and resonance from being designed for a broad mixed audience (150). Agee is not alone in this theory. George Bluestone discusses the similarities between Elizabethan and modern movie audiences in Novels Into Films, and Margaret Farrand Thorp declares that movies seem to be as capable of proceeding on two levels as Elizabethan tragedy: poetry and psychology for the gentleman's gallery, and action and blood
96
for the pit.

Whether regretting the audience's middle-class tastes or upholding its Elizabethan robustness, Agee felt strongly that the

---

96
    America at the Movies (New Haven, 1939), p. 23. Arthur Penn's
Bonnie and Clyde, a popular and critical success, effectively proceeds
on the two levels of visual poetry and psychology; and action and
blood.

artist-audience relationship is inter-penetrating. In the review

of Shoeshine, he stated that qualities such as directness,

magnanimity, even rashness, can hardly exist in a film unless the

makers are sure they are at one with a large, eager, realistic

audience. If this understanding exists, the creative artist is

stimulated to surpass himself. Conversely, if the audience is in a

general state of apathy or anxiety, the creative faculty is reduced,

after a series of rebuffed efforts, to only a small portion of its

potential (279). The attrition, of course, would relate only to the

artist's future endeavors.

The film artist needs contact with his audience. He can become

corrupted by pandering to an audience or by habitually making

esoteric films for art-houses. Agee believed that any loss or

disregard of audiences results in either arrogance or artiness (190).

For decades an inferior, mass art, the film has undergone profound

changes in the past twenty years. Richard Schickel warns that there

is a danger of the film in the 1960's becoming an arid, private thing,

appealing only to the knowledgeable.[97] What Agee feared for a minute

fraction of the film world of the 1940's today may be a possible

threat to the traditional popular role of the medium.

The change in film audiences over the past three decades has

been graphic. The English theatre critic Mr. St. John Ervine wrote

in the early 1930's, not without some validity, that, "If I refer to

film fans as celluloid nit-wits, I do not imply that film fans are

---

[97] Schickel, p. 162.

certifiable lunatics: I do imply that they are people with a low
intellectual standard."[98] Hollis Alpert notes that in his years of
film-reviewing, he has witnessed a profound change in film audiences.
They have grown tired of the Hollywood staples and have shown a
surprising degree of sophistication.[99] Charles Allen Oakley completes
this picture.

> The new cinema, it seems, is catering to people
> with adult minds in contrast to the old cinema
> which was concerned with juvenile minds. One
> critic observed that in the 1920's films were
> generally looked on as a low form of entertainment.
> Now they are the intellectual's delight.[100]

Today, the older generation, who was raised in the happy days when
"films" were called "movies," and going to them was a low-brow
amusement or a generally harmless vice, is baffled by both the academic
interest in films and the passionate involvement of the younger
generation with this "art".[101]

While admitting the validity of Schickel's warning against this
type of decay possible in the art houses, Agee would welcome the
increased sophistication and intelligence of film audiences.

---

[98] Raymond Spottiswoode, A Grammar of the Film (Berkeley, 1965), p.311.

[99] Alpert, p. 238. In 1968, Mike Nichols' The Graduate, a film sympathetic to the younger generation's rejection of the vacuousness of middle class American materialism, is expected to become Hollywood's all-time money-maker.

[100] Oakley, pp. 228-229.

[101] Eleanor Lester, "Shaking the World with an 8-mm. Camera," The New York Times Magazine (November 26, 1967), pp. 45-60.

Opportunities to tap some of the potentialities of the medium, which
he specified twenty years ago, have been opened to serious film-makers.
In the late 1960's, the limitations which Agee viewed as retarding
the development of the film exist in abated form. Within the next
few decades, the remaining obstacles will appear as out-dated as the
other object of his polemics, the Hays Office.

CHAPTER II

THE FILM STYLE OF POETIC REALISM

An innate flexibility prevented Agee from formulating critical
decrees and dogmas in the manner of Andrew Sarris or Siegfried
Kracauer. Yet there can be discerned, from a careful analysis of his
entire critical output, a preference for one particular film style,
which may be termed poetic realism. This mode of rendering reality
occurs when an artist is able to extract the poetry which exists _in_
reality, rather than decorating reality with poetry. Since poetic
realism, in this sense, is central to Agee's esthetic, it is the
subject of investigation in this chapter.

Agee believes that a film director has the capacity, by means of
the motion picture camera, of dealing directly with "unaltered
reality."[1] In no other art form, except in the related field of
photography, is a scientific instrument employed in this way to
transfer a segment of reality.[2] The film artist, however, does not

---

[1]
A Way of Seeing (New York, 1965), p. 4.

[2]
An exception to Agee's statement, made originally in an essay
written in the 1940's, is the work of the avant-garde musical composer
Milton Babbitt. By means of the Columbia-Princeton R.C.A. Electronic
Sound Synthesizer, a massive, enormously expensive computer, he can
precisely reproduce any sound. Babbitt and some other "Zen Electronic"
composers have been utilizing this scientific instrument in their
electronic compositions. One has only to hear Babbitt's "Composition
for Synthesizer" to realize the highly abstract and stylized quality
of the music, most unlike Agee's concept of the unaltered reality
transferred by a camera.

merely record. He must possess the sensibility to be able to perceive that in reality which is aesthetic enough to record. Agee does not maintain that the film can precisely transcribe reality, since he realizes that a camera through the eye of an operator can "lie." He does argue that the film, of all art forms, least alters reality in the process of its transference to an audience.

A score of other film theorists, in addition to Agee, have acknowledged the film's power in transmitting a sense of reality. V. I. Pudovkin, with more declamation than explanation, avers that the film is "par excellence the art form capable of maximum capture of living reality in direct representation."[3] Hollis Alpert suggests that a self-induced form of hypnosis in the viewer enables the film to "provide the greatest illusion of reality."[4] Luis Buñuel explains the cinema's power to create an illusion, perhaps as no other art, in psychological terms: the motion pictures act directly upon the spectator, offering him concrete persons and things, and isolating him, through silence and darkness, from his usual atmosphere.[5] And, according to Marshall McLuhan, the film form manages to approximate real life to a stunning degree by means of its extraordinary powers of

---

[3]
V. I. Pudovkin, Film Technique and Film Acting (New York, 1960), p. 250.

[4]
Hollis Alpert, The Dreams and the Dreamers (New York, 1962), p. 220.

[5]
Luis Buñuel, "A Statement," in Film Makers on Film Making, ed. Harry M. Geduld (Bloomington, 1967), p. 175.

6
illusion.

In spite of all of the claims, at times exaggerated, for the
illusion of reality in the film, it is, after all, relative. Even with
its affinity for realism, and its technical and scientific resources,
the film can not record reality without imperfections. An impression
of depth, for instance, is lacking in all except some of the
experimental films. Spatially, the screen discloses a flat world
reduced to a single plane, limited by the frame which surrounds it. In
addition, other more technical spatial and temporal differences exist
between the real world and the film world. [7] Agee recognizes that
reality, as represented in the film, must be treated as distinct from
actual reality. The director's task is to discover, from an artistic
perspective, what is more real than the actual, and what is less
real (223).

The sense of reality in a film should not be confused with the
use of non-actors, or with a semi-documentary approach, or with any of
the other "realistic" trappings. Darryl F. Zanuck's Wilson is an
instance of such an artistic blurring: The makers of the film copied
all of the cracks in the original portraits of Presidents in the White
House and even studied 160,000 feet of relevant newsreel footage, but
the film is unconvincing (112). Agee charges that this type of

---

6
Marshall McLuhan, Understanding Media: the Extensions of Man
(New York, 1964), p. 290.

7
For a thorough technical analysis, see Ralph Stephenson and Jean
R. Debrix, The Cinema as Art (Baltimore, 1965) pp. 32-36; 123-138.

pseudo-realism can smother a feeling of reality as readily as it can liberate it. The form of realism consistently admired is what Michelangelo Antonioni terms "interior realism," a rendering of reality based on individual feelings or relationships between individuals, instead of the accumulation and presentation of a mass of detail.[8]

In Agee's terms, the degree of reality in a film can in large part be determined by the incidence of non-distortion and "excess of energy." Director Vincente Minelli distorted reality in Meet Me In St. Louis by an attempt to refurbish, rather than honor, it. The idea of the girls' fear of relocating in New York could have been realized artistically if Minelli had committed to the screen the girls' visual and emotional milieu.[9] A director can communicate reality without distortion only if he respects it. Agee notes with pleased surprise that the wounded men in Since You Went Away actually appeared wounded (351). Conversely, the typical Hollywood distortion of reality is described in a review of the film Albuquerque.

> An actor, shot at, grabs his kneecap and falls
> down the stairs. Within a few seconds he is
> able to explain, in a politely stoical voice,
> that he isn't badly hurt -- just hit in the leg.
> This is a fair measure of how intimately most
> movies are acquainted with even the most

---

[8] Milton S. Davis, "Most Controversial Director," The New York Times (November 15, 1964), pp. 34-35; 104-114.

[9] James Agee, Agee on Film: Reviews and Comments (New York, 1958), p. 127. All further references, which will be set in parentheses in the text, are to this edition.

> rudimentary realities of experience. A good
> excruciating crack on every kneecap that needs
> it might be enough to revolutionize Hollywood.
> Even if it didn't, it would be a pleasure to
> deliver (294).

Other commentators on Agee have noted his insistence that
non-distortion is essential to the depiction of reality, but Norman
Holland goes too far. He states that when Agee calls for realism
he means honesty.[10] In Agee's criticism, honesty denotes an absence
of its opposite vice, intentional deceit. Realism does mean
faithfulness to the realities of experience, rather than honesty.
There can be no argument, however, about his consistent commitment
to the communication of reality, as Peter Ohlin points out: "The
heart of Agee's criticism is its insistence on the uniqueness and
sacredness of human reality."[11]

"Excess of energy" is a term Agee first employs in reviewing
Malraux's Man's Hope, a film imbued with the strongest possible sense
of reality. Conceived by Eisenstein, the principle of excess of
energy essentially refers to the intrusion of ostensibly irrelevant --
but actually highly relevant -- bits of business into a film. A
guerilla's sudden skipping change in step or his sudden hand to his
sweating neck, or a dog walking in from one side of the frame while
a ball idly rolls in from the other side, are illustrative moments

---

10
"Agee on Film: Reviewer Re-Viewed," Hudson Review, XII (Spring
1959), 148-151. Both Ohlin and Behar, in their dissertations on Agee,
accept this inaccurate equation of realism with honesty.

11
"James Agee: A Critical Study" (Ann Arbor, 1964), pp. 178-179.

of this kind of action in <u>Man's Hope</u>. To Agee, these little
happenings brilliantly lock men and their efforts and feelings into an
exact real place and time (240). The embodiment of this principle in
a film can convey the urgency and power of the real. George Rouquier's
<u>Farrebique</u>, the visual embodiment in subject and temperament of Agee's
<u>Let Us Now Praise Famous Men</u>, is another rare achievement of this type
of rendering of reality. Rouquier dares to include "casual scraps of
existence," which do not in themselves qualify as incident, or even
description, in the sense of revealing mood or character. These
instances are of the essence of being, not studied effects or displays
of camera virtuosity (297). A similiar form of realism is achieved
in <u>The Story of G.I. Joe</u>. Ernie Pyle's sitting on the side of a road
while some soldiers straggle past is one of many seemingly unconnected
parts, "as immediate and as unlimited by thought or prejudice as what
the eye might see on the spot, in a casual glance" (172).

As with some of his other critical theories, Agee consciously
attempted to endow his film scripts with a sense of reality through
excess energy. In <u>Noa Noa</u> during the funeral procession of Pomare,
the last Tahitian King, Agee instructs the camera to record many odd
bits of business: a short man in the band lipping his flute for an
upcoming solo; the village shopkeeper in the crowd discreetly picking
his nose.[12] Because of repeated incidents like these in the scripts,
W. M. Frohock refers to Agee's extraordinary ability "for revealing

[12]
    <u>Agee on Film, Vol. II: Five Film Scripts</u>,(New York, 1958), p. 63.

significance in a gesture, an object, any unobtrusive thing which
seems only to 'happen' to catch the eye."[13]   Though achieved by Agee
and a few other script writers during the 1940's and 1950's, the
excess energy principle has since evolved into a basic practice in
the film language of the 1960's.

An approach to movie-making more orthodox than the excess energy
school is set forth in Béla Balázs' Theory of the Film. He states
that most film-goers do not realize that what they are watching is
the staging of a film script, very much as they would be watching the
staging of a play in the theatre.[14]   Every detail is outlined in
advance, filming is in strict accordance with the script, and
distribution is begun on schedule. In contrast, the modern
improvisatory approach, admired by Agee, is summarized by Federico
Fellini. "I believe that a good picture has to have defects. It has
to have mistakes in it, like life, like people."[15]   To clarify Fellini's
meaning, two examples can be gleaned from La Strada. A horse, not
originally planned for in the script, wanders down the street as
Gelsomina waits forlornly on the curb for Zampano's return.

---

[13]
  "James Agee -- The Question of Wasted Talent," The Novel of
Violence in America (Dallas, 1957), p. 228.

[14]
  Béla Balázs, Theory of the Film, trans. Edith Bone (New York,
1953), p. 246.

[15]
  "The Road Beyond Neorealism," in Film: A Montage of Theories, ed.
Richard Dyer Mac Cann, (New York, 1966)p. 383.

A similar spontaneous occurrence is the sequence of the three musicians gaily playing as they walk along a country road. Gelsomina, who has boldly decided to leave Zampano and strike out on her own, hears and instinctively skips nonchalantly after the musicians. Fellini did not plan to film either of these scenes. The three musicians, just as the horse, were walking by while shooting was in progress. Fellini, one infers from his brief statements, perceived that if these chance happenings were interposed at particular moments in the film, the poignancy of the sequences would be increased. Agee would view such "defects" or "mistakes" as the peripheral chance happenings which create a texture of reality in a film.[16]

Jean Cocteau has also written of these elusive scraps of existence. Having spent hours attempting to capture a certain reflection on the floor in filming The Beauty and the Beast, he sighed that film making entails the laborious task of trying to control chance.[17] If there are "no doors left open to chance," then what Cocteau in this context terms poetry, and what Agee means by the illusion of reality, "which

---

16
  Fellini in one instance was more literal than I have suggested in the context of Agee's criticism: at the end of Nights of Cabiria, when Giulietta Masina is walking down a path through the woods, followed by a band of youthful musicians, an over-head sound microphone is clearly visible at the top of the screen for a split second. This type of "mistake," which does not occur in any other Fellini film, is more Brechtian (since Fellini could have cut it) than improvisatory.

17
  Diary of a Film (New York, 1950), p. 136.

is difficult enough to trap, will certainly be frightened away."[18] The
theory of a flawed, more plausible sense of reality, praised by Agee
and Cocteau in the 1940's, today has become standard operating
procedure in the hand-held cameras of Jean-Luc Godard or an
out-of-focus shot by Agnes Varda. Penelope Houston accurately
appraises this development among the band of critically acclaimed
directors in the 1960's as an attempt to invest films with "the
psychological and visual reality of modern man."[19]

The marked intellectual and artistic milieu of these younger
directors has paralleled the invention of sophisticated cinematic
tools, which can produce not only amazingly lifelike recordings, but
can bring about a heightened perceptual grasp of reality.[20] Despite
these advances, the large commercial studios throughout the world
grind out films, not only lacking in anything approaching the-scraps-
of-existence kind of realism Agee sought, but in fact spawning a world
of pseudo-reality replete with, as Max Kozloff satirically writes,

---

[18]
   Diary of a Film, (New York, 1950), p. 50.

[19]
   The Contemporary Cinema (Baltimore, 1963), p. 186. Compare the
modern folk/rock music of the Beatles and Bob Dylan , whose supremacy
in their field throughout the 1960's has been unquestioned. Both have
cultivated a type of flawed, authentic sound: the Beatles' numerical
count-down before "Taxman" (which could have been erased easily) and
their wild abandonment in "Hey, Jude;" Bob Dylan's irregular breathing
and harmonica playing in all of his work.

[20]
   Slavko Vorkapich, "Toward True Cinema," in *Introduction to the Art
of the Movies* (New York, 1960), p. 294.

"secret agents with genitals of cast iron and singing nannies."[21]
Sadly ironic is the large studios' progression from the Code-enforced
brand of reality to an equally distorted but now exploitative world
of sex and violence, epitomized by James Bond. Agee's advocacy of
excess energy, pioneered by Eisenstein and advanced by Malraux,
Fellini, and others, has not penetrated deeply the high citadels of
film commerce.

In the demand for filmic realism, Agee frequently extolls the
potentialities of the documentary form. In 1943, he prescribed some
British Second World War documentaries, Before The Raid, ABCA, and
Psychiatry in Action, for those who, at that dire time, were talking
of the need for "escape." The force of reality is communicated, in
certain documentaries like these, with power, beauty, chaos; there is,
in effect, no distortion. Agee believes there is no better "escape"
than this type of cathartic encounter with aesthetic reality (58).

One of the main advantages of the documentary is its ability to
enable viewers to see feelingly. The 1939 The City saliently
represents a documentary which achieves the full potential of its
form. Because of masterful techniques, it enables many viewers to
experience what it is like to be trapped in a city traffic jam, or to
live in a crowded tenement house.[22] Agee pays tribute to the man most

21
"Le Bonheur," Film Quarterly, XX (Winter 1966-67), 35-37.

22
Gloria Waldron, The Information Film (New York, 1964), p. 29.

responsible for infusing a sense of reality into the documentary form,
Robert Flaherty, who transformed the genre from a series of dull,
factual films, usually travelogues with patronizing glimpses of exotic
peoples in far-off places, to vivid records brimming with the drama of
man struggling against his environment.[23]   It is while watching
Flaherty's Nanook of the North that some in the audience flinch when
Nanook licks an icy blade. Knowing that Nanook is an Eskimo, who
routinely performs such tasks, seems to elicit more of a response than
would a purely fictional portrayal.

Another distinct characteristic of the documentary form is
similar in theory to Agee's "excess energy." The documentary approach
attempts to capture the exceptions and nuances of behaviour, such as
the particular way a man smokes. A shot of a group of people at a ball
game, for instance, will invariably include one person who for some
reason is looking away.[24]   Incidents like the guerilla's sudden change
in step in Man's Hope contribute to the appearance of reality in a film.
Akira Kurosawa incorporates this documentary device into his highly
realistic fictional films. In Sanjuro he focuses on three men stepping
across a small brook with a stone in the middle. Only one of the three
men steps on the stone going one way; seconds later on their return, all
three avoid the stone. This minor sequence in itself has no symbolic
significance, nor any relationship to character, theme, or plot

---

[23]
"Old Master," Time, LI (September 20, 1948), 94-100. Unsigned
review by Agee.

[24]
Waldron, p. 26.

development. In capturing the exceptions and nuances of behaviour,
Kurosawa communicates in his films the randomness and specificity of
reality.

Agee realizes that although the documentary form has certain
positive factors, it is not inherently superior to, truer, or nobler
than the fiction film. The documentary deals with non-human objects
and processes, and if human beings are included, they are shown in
relation to their offices and functions, not with respect to their
qualities and relationships as individuals. Hence the documentary
denies itself the identification process, which not only gives the
audience its deepest emotional experience, but is also important for
the commercial life of a film.[25] Within these confines, however, as
Pare Lorentz and Robert Flaherty have demonstrated, artistic
achievements are attainable.

These restrictions have proved insuperable to some directors, and
Agee records the failures in and special temptations of the form. He
notes that, in practice, the average documentary is often as "dismally
hostile to reality as most fiction films" (237). The kindest epithet
for the typical documentary is "dull," because too many of its
producers "confuse reality with fact." They mistakenly believe that
a factual record is sufficient, since photofact is inherently superior
to film fiction (94). Agee cautions, as he does in connection with

[25]
Ivor Montagu, Film World (Middlesex, 1964), p. 285. The display of
technical virtuosity and imagination in Stanley Kubrick's A Space
Odyssey: 2001 is so stunning that this fictional film is proving
commercially successful, even though it affords no appreciable character
identification.

the art houses, that the makers of documentaries are vulnerable to temptations and liabilities as serious as those imposed by rankest commercialism. Freed from commercial worries, the producers of documentaries can fall prey to didacticism. As a result, much of the pedagogical and social content in documentaries reveals special pleading and faulty reasoning (308).

Agee believes the solution to these problems is a hybrid form. Robert Flaherty achieved success in molding material, rather than in slavishly recording fact. Flaherty preferred a freer documentary form in order to convey the impression of reality. For Nanook of the North, Flaherty followed the Eskimo Nanook with a camera for two months hoping to get a picture of his harpooning a seal through a breathing hole in the ice. Finally a dead seal had to be used for the sequence. Lines were rigged to it under the ice, and a group of Eskimos out of camera range pulled on the lines while Nanook on camera struggled with the harpooned seal. Another acclaimed documentary of Flaherty's is Man of Aran, which concerns the poverty-stricken fishermen on the island of Aran. The climax is a hunt of the basking shark to obtain oil for islanders' lamps. When Flaherty made the film, these fishermen had not killed a shark for sixty years; they had to be taught by a fisherman imported by Flaherty. The islanders, as a matter of record, had had electric light on the island for many years.[26] Agee would unhesitatingly commend Flaherty's creative handling of

---

[26]
Montagu, p. 283.

material, as he would endorse his pronouncement, "One often has to
distort a thing to catch its true spirit."[27]

William Wellman's The Story of G.I. Joe represents a substantive
fusion of fictional and documentary techniques. It makes the fictional
elements ring with the sound of fact, and, in Agee's judgment, far more
intimate and expressive fact than it is possible to record on the
spot (174). Though there is inherent meaning in fact, an artist's
intelligence, and not just a camera's recording power, is necessary
for art. Malraux's Man's Hope achieves "inspired documentation,"
since it is at once factual and symbolic.[28] Agee writes that the films
he most eagerly looks forward to are not the typical, factual
documentaries, but "works of pure fiction, played against, and into,
and in collaboration with unrehearsed and uninvented reality" (237).

A lyric or creative documentary, essentially what Agee demands,
is a paradox. Yet there is evidence of such attempts throughout the
history of the film . In Germany in the 1920's, Walter Ruttmann
served his apprenticeship under the Russian director Dziga Vertov, a
practitioner who was of the extreme factual school of documentary.
Ruttmann experimented with and expanded the form, wanting to surprise
life with his camera. His stated interest was not in divulging news
items, but in composing "optical music" or lyric documentaries. His

---

[27]
    Quoted but not identified in A. R. Fulton, Motion Pictures
(Oklahoma, 1960), p. 186.

[28]
    "The New Pictures," Time, XLIX (February 3, 1947), 93-95.

1929 <u>Man with the Movie Camera</u> has been acclaimed the successful
result of such experiments.[29] Further, the father of the British
documentary, John Grierson, demanded a "creative treatment of
actuality." A documentary to him was more than an actual
representation of life; it was an interpretation. And in so far as
it had a narrative as well as a unified theme, it resembled a
fictional film.[30] With this outlook, Grierson did not hesitate to
pose his subjects for special effects.[31] These examples and
definitions parallel Agee's treatment of the documentary as a viable
source for more immediacy and realism in the film medium.

Since Agee's time, there have been sporadic connections between
fiction and the documentary. The British Film Institute in the late
1950's sponsored a group of promising young directors, who experimented
with films partaking of fictional and documentary elements. The
experiment, known as Free Cinema, became a significant new movement
in the production of feature films.[32] Tony Richardson, its most
celebrated alumnus, directed <u>The Loneliness of the Long Distance</u>

---

[29]
Siegfried Kracauer, <u>From Caligari to Hitler</u> (Princeton, 1947),
p. 185, makes a perceptive psychological study of German documentaries
and fictional films during the 1920's and 1930's.

[30]
Fulton, p. 183.

[31]
Ernest Callenbach, "Looking Backward," <u>Film Quarterly</u>,XXII (Fall
1968), 1-10.

[32]
Charles Allen Oakley, <u>Where We Came In</u> (London, 1964), p. 217.

Runner and A Taste of Honey, fiction films set in the documentary
terms of stark, unembellished actual locations, straight camera
recording, and grainy, non-glossy, film stock. From such virile
achievements, the documentary-fiction film in the 1960's seems to be
returning to the extremes of the Dzia Vertov school. John
Cassavetes' Shadows, a miscegenation story, and Lionel Rogosin's
Come Back, Africa, a story of apartheid, have no ostensible plot,
no character development, no unified theme. The characters are told
to live their lives in front of a camera.[33] Since Agee dismisses
the factual, usually dull, approach of the straight documentary, I
believe he would find this development too self-limiting and,
ultimately, self-defeating. This method, contrasted with
Richardson's, does not draw upon the resources inherent either in
the documentary or in fiction.

Filmic treatment of the war in Vietnam, one of the gravest
problems in the world over the past four years, is revealing. The
rash of recent straight, "live" documentaries on the war, like
Eugene S. Jones' A Face of War, evidence continuation of the trend
toward purely factual documentation. Jones, a news cameraman, spent
ninety-seven days of combat with a Marine platoon in Vietnam. At
the other pole stands the only Hollywood fictional treatment of the
Vietnam war, John Wayne's The Green Berets, which is in the
tradition of commercial exploitation.[34] This time, by a play on

[33]
Montagu, p. 285

[34] See Chapter I, p.45, for a full treatment of Hollywood's practice
of commercial exploitation.

violence, the exploitation is carried out in the name of patriotism.
Thus, no treatment of the war to date has been able to draw upon the
strength of both documentary and fictional techniques.

The documentary has had an abiding impact on the development of
the film. The two most important revolts in film history, Soviet
expressive realism of the 1920's and Italian neo-realism of the 1940's,
revolved around a documentary style. Expressive realism denotes the
extensions of realism made by Pudovkin's plastic expressiveness,
Eisenstein's dynamic editing, and Dovzhenko's intense stylization.
"Neo-realism" was used for the Italian films because of the German
"street films" of the 1920's (Murnau's The Last Laugh, Pabst's The
Joyless Street, E. A. Dupont's Variety), which treated the life of the
common man with a high degree of realism.

Agee's admiration for the Russian films was as evident as his
immediate and full acceptance of the first films of Italian neo-realism.
He saw in these Italian films a fulfillment of the documentary-fiction
promise.

Agee classified Open City and Shoeshine, the first neo-realist
films distributed in this country, exceptional artistic achievements.
Shoeshine was judged to be as beautiful, moving, and heartening a
film as one is ever likely to see (274). He compared the sharp
excitement and spirit of Open City with the "libertarian jubilation
of excitement under which it was all but inevitable that men like
Eisenstein and Dovzhenko and Pudovkin should make some of the
greatest works of art of this century" (195). Agee admired in both
Italian films the special brand of realism, enriched and
intensified by the "poetry" which resides in the depths

of reality.[35]

Federico Fellini, who still considers himself in the neo-realist tradition, states that neo-realism does not consist in showing what happens in the everyday world, but in "the power to condense, to show the essence of things."[36]   Cesare Zavattini, script writer for da Sica's Shoeshine and Bicycle Thief, declares his intention of wanting to make things as they are, almost by themselves as it were, create their own special significance: "to analyze fact so deeply that we see things we have never noticed before."[37]   Neo-realism, then, essentially fulfills Agee's desire that films burrow into the core of reality.

Although its direct force was spent by the early 1950's, neo-realism has had a substantial effect on the subsequent development of the film. The neo-realist influence on Satyajit Ray, one of the foremost contemporary directors, has been technical as well as thematic. His Apu trilogy relentlessly depicts the raw, oppressive

---

[35]
   The New York film critics, John Mason Brown, Manny Farber, John McCarten, and Bosley Crowther, praised Open City in 1946. The film was a welcome relief from the bulk of Hollywood glossy products of that era, but compared to some of the better films of the 1960's, its impact pales. It is remembered today as a solid achievement rather than, as Agee (with characteristic over-praise) termed it, a film comparable to the works of Eisenstein and the greatest works of art of the century. None of the other New York critics went to this extreme.

[36]
   "The Road Beyond Neorealism," in Film: A Montage of Theories, ed. Richard Dyer Mac Cann, p. 380.

[37]
   "Some Ideas on the Cinema," in Film: A Montage of Theories, ed. Richard Dyer Mac Cann, p. 216.

social conditions of Bengal. He insisted for his first film on the
use of natural backgrounds, instead of the artificial studio sets, and
on the maximum use of non-actors. He particularly avoided familar
star faces, and, to achieve a greater sense of immediacy and reality,
he intentionally employed an inexperienced cameraman.[38]   Ray also
followed his Italian predecessors in post-synchronizing the sound
track. Though dialogue was recorded on location, it was used as a
guide in the recording of the final sound track, made under
acoustically controlled conditions.[39]   In the finest tradition of
neo-realism, he produced his first picture, Pather Panchali (1961) on
the kind of shoestring budget Agee advocated in a 1946 review.

Jack Behar states that Agee admired neo-realism because of its
function of recording, even memorializing, what human beings have
lived through. These films, however, according to Behar, do not
"interpret, reorder, or redefine reality."[40]   If this were true, I
am certain that Agee would have levelled the same charge at them as

38
    An inexperienced cameraman guarantees nothing: as a conscious
choice, it seems as shaky as Agee's insistence on thinking of himself
as an amateur critic, a belief he set forth in his first review for
the Nation (December 26, 1942), and never renounced or amended. John
Updike, "No Use Talking," New Republic, CXLVII (August 13, 1962), 23-24,
justly upraids Agee for this pointless belief in amateurism.

39
    Erik Barnouw and S. Krishnaswamy, Indian Film (New York, 1963),
pp. 221-222.

40
    "James Agee: The World of His Work" (Ann Arbor, 1963), pp. 96-97.
An unpublished dissertation from Ohio State University.

he did at the straight, "dull" documentaries, which do not go beyond
accurate recording. That the neo-realist films interpret reality by
penetrating it deeply enough is their principal achievement, the one
which, more than any other, elicited Agee's admiration.

One of the factors most responsible for infusing realism into
these films is the use of non-actors. Open City, with a successful
blend of professional and non-professional actors, contains acting
which almost perfectly defines "the poetic-realistic root of attitude
from which the grand trunk of movies at their best would have to grow"
(195). The fierce poetic spirit of this film fuses with its
documentary realism to form a style which realizes many of the
possibilities inherent in the medium. Such realism, however, would
be immeasurably more difficult to obtain with professional, world-
renowned, "star" actors. Agee argues that Hollywood's system in the
1930's and 1940's tended to diminish the film's power for creating an
illusion of reality. John Garfield, for example, became so familiar
in the tough-man role that his mere presence threatened an audience's
capacity for belief.[41] The likes of John Garfield, John Wayne, and
Bette Davis constituted Hollywood's version of reality. Except in the
frankest kind of myth, like a Western, such actors can destroy a film's
sense of reality. This is most evident in a film attempting to depict
"real" people, like the Henry Fonda portrayal of Tom Joad in The
Grapes of Wrath.

---

[41]
   "The Postman Always Rings Twice," Time, XLVII (May 6, 1946), 96-100.

Hollywood's star-system, conceived and nurtured for commercial
reasons, often proved ludicrously inadequate in attempting to
establish plausibility. Agee notes wryly that with all of the
competent Chinese actors in California, a glittering list of
Occidental stars was nevertheless engaged to portray the Chinese
roles in Dragon Seed: "I shan't even try to say how awful and silly
they looked -- Miss Hepburn especially, in her shrewdly tailored,
Peck and Peckish pajamas" (110). Colin Young points out with some
humor that we as members of an audience cannot believe in the end of
the world watching such heroes and heroines as Gregory Peck and Ava
Gardner. We know we shall see them again, and as the message of On
the Beach is telegraphed, we are reaching for our coats, not searching
our consciences.[42] We wonder what Peck's next movie will be, and
whether this time he will get the girl and keep her.[43]

Agee's alternative to Hollywood's system is a judicious use of
non-actors. He calls for the institution of this practice on a broad
scale. Although Hollywood in the mid 1940's risked the hazards of
location-shooting, it made no parallel attempts with the use of

---

[42]
Colin Young, like Agee and other critics, is speculating about
audience reaction. Although the actual effects cannot be reasonably
estimated, except by the individual, the critics are discussing one
Hollywood practice, which does have a bearing on audience reaction.

[43]
"Nobody Dies," in Film: Book 2, Films of Peace and War, ed.
Robert Hughes (New York, 1962), p. 93.

non-actors. Jimmy Stewart, even in a real location, remains instantly
recognizable as Jimmy Stewart. Agee calls attention to the effects
attainable when film makers are bold enough to cast non-actors and
then, "leave the rest to the reverent, simple acting of real, deeply
moved, everyday human beings."[44] He advances the classic argument
for the use of non-actors, enunciated by Pudovkin in the 1920's, that
directors should cast the perfect people rather than the perfect
actors (132). Admittedly, this casting by type is beset with
difficulties, but not without the compensatory factor of heightening
the illusion of reality.

In assessing a collection of Agee's Reviews, Stanley Kauffmann
is generally favorable except in this particular area.

> At bottom he has, I believe, little regard for or
> understanding of the art of acting; indeed through-
> out this collection there are numerous references
> to his preference for well-directed non-professionals
> as against actors. This, to me, is a blindness, a
> literalness puzzling in a man of his imagination . . .
> The fact that fine directors like da Sica have made
> memorable films with non-actors doesn't really prove
> Agee's theory. Umberto D, moving as it is, would
> have been infinitely better with a good actor in
> the title role.[45]

Besides the fact that the title role in Umberto D was played by a
professional actor, Carlo Battisti, Kauffmann's main objection is
invalid. Agee repeatedly demonstrates his appreciation of the
artistry of a Walter Huston or a Laurence Olivier or a Charles Chaplin.

---

[44]
"Documentaries Grow Up," Time, XLII (September 13, 1943), 94-95.

[45]
"Life in Reviews," New Republic, CXXXIX (December 1, 1958), 18-19.

On the other hand, Kauffmann does focus on one of the less tenable positions in the criticism. In crusading for a greater sense of reality in the films of the 1940's, Agee justifiably rebelled against the mediocre actors who were groomed into stardom, not the great actors, like Laurence Olivier, who either surmount the obstacle of familiarity and wrench belief from audiences, or dazzle them with virtuosity. Yet some of Agee's bald statements concerning "professional" actors like John Garfield, can be misleading if not understood in the entire context of his criticism. In essence, he saw no future for the medium as long as it was so dependent on star personalities. Is anyone's capacity for belief strong enough to accept Gregory Peck as Captain Ahab (considering Mr. Peck's acting ability)? Ironically, Agee, years prior to the filming of Moby Dick, placed his strongest hopes for Hollywood in John Huston, the director responsible for casting Gregory Peck as Ahab.

Agee prefers an acting style consistent with his belief in poetic realism. He describes the non-actors' achievement in Malraux's Man's Hope as something "beyond acting and utterly different from it" (240). He singles out the peasant who, in a plane for the first time, can not locate a flying field because of the strange, new perspective from the air. This bit of action represents an inspired blending of realism with imagination: realism partly because the peasant, not Oscar Homolka, is unknown; imagination because the awesome burden of responsibility is too much for the simple peasant, whose face reveals the consequent tragic disintegration he undergoes. The portrayal of German officers -- no Helmut Dantines -- in Open City is

likewise lauded for being strongly felt and "poetically stylized."
This is the same compounding, with different terms, of realism and
poetry. Agee occasionally perceives such an achievement in a
professional performance. Ingrid Bergman's portrayal of Maria, in
For Whom the Bell Tolls,[46] is termed a "blend of poetic grace with
quiet realism" (47).

An ironic postscript to Agee's preference for non-actors is the
inordinate demands he made of actors in his own film scripts. The
scene in Noa-Noa which describes Gauguin's painting Tehura, his future
mistress, includes these instructions: "In a purely aesthetic way
he is deeply moved by what he sees, and is doing and learning; this
emotion is 'cold, sad, impersonal, tender'; it also carries in it
gaiety and a curious kind of anger or delight."[47] Equally impossible
for realization are the directions at the conclusion of The Blue Hotel.
After the Swede has been killed, the Easterner reveals that Johnnie
was indeed cheating. The Easterner is then left alone in the saloon
with the dead Swede.

> With the absolute silence an even more fierce
> and living quiet intensifies in the Easterner's
> face and becomes, as well, sorrow, pity,
> tenderness, a passionate desire for, and hope-
> lessness of, expiation. The face rises on a
> high wave of realization, almost transfigured,
> on the verge, even, of mysticism, yet iron,

---

[46]
Agee's detailed analysis of Ingrid Bergman's performance in this
film demonstrates his understanding of the art of acting, and in part
refutes Kauffmann's charge.

[47]
Agee on Film, Vol. II: Five Film Scripts, pp. 76-77.

> virile, tragic -- as, very slowly, his eyes
> still fixed toward the Swede, he walks into
> extreme CLOSE UP.[48]

Agee's Southern prose ardor, combined with his sensitive imagination,
could detail such complex instructions, which are more in the nature
of literary character descriptions than cinematic directions for
actors. The film critic who calls for natural, untrained non-actors
in order to heighten a film's illusion of reality set down in his own
scripts patently unrealistic guides.

Realism, whether documentary or neo-realistic, or in part
arising from a judicious use of non-actors, constitutes half of Agee's
preferred film style. The other essential is poetry,[49] which, when
wedded to realism, results in "poetic realism -- the dead center of
most good cinema." Agee observes, without elaboration, that this
style is almost a natural Russian characteristic.[50] V. I. Pudovkin, in
analyzing Sergei Eisenstein's Potemkin, defines what, I believe, Agee
had in mind. From the shatteringly bloody, realistic sequence on the
Odessa steps, Eisenstein progressed to "free, symbolic representation,
independent of the requirements of elementary probability" in the
firing of the rebel battleship upon the Odessa Theatre. By montage,
this firing appears to cause the stone lions atop the theatre to rise

---

[48]
Agee on Film, Vol. II: Five Film Scripts, p. 488.

[49]
The term "poetry" is used broadly to connote the indirect, non-
realistic modes like suggestion, symbolism, allegory, and fantasy.

[50]
"People's Avengers," Time, XLIV (July 10, 1944), 94-96.

in indignation and roar. [51] Realism and poetry are not only compatible in the same film, they can, in the hands of a film artist like Eisenstein, underline and intensify each other.

Russian expressive realism, however, is only one approach to realizing the fullest potential of the medium. From a free interplay between harsh realism and symbolic interpretation, Agee envisions the further feat of perceiving the poetry which exists within reality. He often notes the camera's capacity for recording actual existence, and the director who resists temptations to alter or improve on the actual can communicate the poetic vitality of what exists in front of his camera.[52] This theory is enunciated in the review of the British war fiction film The Raider. The most realistic, "documentary" material is presented without rhetoric or comment, but with such a deep and unpretentious sense of its ultimate meanings, that it becomes "automatically poetic" (224). Poetry does not have to be added onto reality. A true artist can extract the poetry within reality.

Agee seldom commends an achievement in this regard. An exception is the final scene in Malraux's Man's Hope, which involves the crash of Loyalist flyers and the slow, painfully realistic bringing down of the dead and wounded from mountaintop to valley, while more and more peasants join both to offer assistance and to mourn. Agee praises Malraux's

[51]
Pudovkin, p. 117.

[52]
Farrebique," Time, LI (March 15, 1948), 100-104.

interlocking of fact and symbol in this scene, which culminates in a colossal dirge for heroes:

> The descent of the broken heroes from the desperate stone crown of Spain, as from a Cross, to the maternal valley, a movement so conceived that a whole people and a whole terrain become one sorrowing and triumphal Pieta for twentieth-century man . . . (241-242).

Malraux, by penetrating deeply enough into the meaning of an airplane crash, made this common wartime occurrence assume symbolic proportions.

Georges Rouquier plumbed a similar poetic depth in Farrebique by allowing his camera to record the mysterious beauty of nature and rural man. He portrayed the daily chores and the normal cyclical happenings so simply that the incandescence of poetry shines through the communicated reality. "This realism is as distinct from the stodgy realism of documentaries as the poetry is distinct from the sickly prettiness of most 'art' movies."[53] Jean Vigo's "Zero de Conduite," with its occasional glimpses of naturalistic action as "grim and firm as stone outcrops," is classified as another of the few great movie poems. Although Agee only lightly sketches his appreciation, I would cite, in substantiation of his claim, the fact that the film's realistic surface explodes unexpectedly with symbolic, purely expressionistic moments. The midget principal unjustly shouting at the shy boy (as subjectively imagined by the boy, but objectively projected onto the screen), the pillow fight in the boys' dormitory, and the slow-motion procession of the crucified teacher have a sharp

---

[53] "Farrebique," Time, LI (March 15, 1948), 100-104.

realistic edge and yet are unfettered flights of anarchic imagination.

In the history of the film, one of the outstanding examples of poetic realism is D. W. Griffith's The Birth of a Nation. Often praised for its realism, it does create powerfully realistic scenes, but Agee believes it also has mythological depths, touching upon the memory and imagination of entire peoples. The homecoming of the defeated hero, the rapist and his victim among the dark leaves, the dead young soldiers after a battle, all partake of a "dream-like absoluteness"; all are etched in the strongest terms of realism and yet far surpass it. Agee suspects that Griffith achieved this fusion instinctively, never fully comprehending its potential: "He doesn't appear ever to have realized one of the richest promises that movies hold, as the perfect medium for realism raised to the level of high poetry" (313-315).

One of the most recent as well as most satisfying movements in the film is the new Czechoslovak cinema. Jan Kadar's The Shop on Main Street, Jiri Menzel's Closely Watched Trains, Ivan Passer's Intimate Lighting, and Milos Forman's Loves of a Blonde and The Firemans Ball, one of the most acclaimed films shown at the 1968 Lincoln Center Film Festival, have received international critical and popular recognition. These films sensitively, simply portray, in the words of Passer, "life as it is, unheroic, unexceptional but nonetheless interesting."[54] They observe small human aspirations in terms of gentle poignancy and quiet poetry. Milos Forman, who acknowledges

---

[54] "The Eyes Have It," Time, (September 23, 1966), p. 74.

his debt to the Italian neo-realists, works with a careful balance
of professional actors and handpicked amateurs, and uses actual
locations as well as some of the other documentary techniques.[55] This
Czech development is the most complete realization to date of Agee's
desire for poetic realism, the style he believed to be best suited to
the film medium.

Ever since the dichotomy between Lumière and Méliès, some film
theorists have contended that realism and poetry should be treated as
separate entities. George Bluestone believes the two tendencies
should remain separate, since they can act as checks on each other and
thus assure a balance in film production. Bound by the realistic
demands of the photographed object on the one hand, and on the other
by the formative principle of editing, the film alternates endlessly
between documentary realism and spatial fantasy.[56] Agee maintains that
the fertile life of the film is not in the separation and balance
accepted by Bluestone, but in the fusion of realism and poetry, in the
intermingling of fact and symbol even though, at times, they have been
declared antagonistic. Jean Cocteau most felicitiously described this
union in praising his cameraman for at last, after prodding, being
able to capture "a sort of supernatural quality within the limits of
realism; which is the reality of childhood. The fairyland without

[55] Jan Zalman, "Question Marks on the New Czechoslovak Cinema," Film
Quarterly XXI (Winter 1967-68), 18-27.

[56] Novels Into Films (Berkeley, 1966), p. 217.

fairies."[57]

A few commentators on Agee have been blinded by his insistence
on the necessity of realism in films. Richard Griffith, former
curator of the Museum of Modern Art Film Library, writes that Agee's
love for the film endowed him with an insight into the nature of the
film medium perhaps deeper than any other American. "What he saw was
that the movie medium is a photographic medium, and that it was the
potentialities of photography, rather than of the devices borrowed
from theatre and literature which need to be explored."[58] This
estimation is only partially accurate, since it sets forth Agee's
position on realism, but fails to mention his equal insistence on
poetry. Norman Holland is grievously short-sighted in charging that
Agee's demand for real people and real locations is too limiting:
Agee's view "totally rules out films that work allegorically, westerns,
melodramas, horror or science-fiction films, or, to put it bluntly,
most movies." Further, it is alleged that Agee indiscriminately
praised any semi-documentary based on real incidents, shot in a real
locale, or created by non-professionals.[59] In addition to contrary
evidence already presented, an in-depth analysis of Agee's theories
on the wide filmic possibilities in the field of the poetic will not

57
  Cocteau, p. 149.

58
  Review of Agee on Film: Reviews and Comments, New York Times Book
Review (November 16, 1958), p. 5.

59
  "Agee on Film: Reviewer Re-Viewed," Hudson Review, XII (Spring
1959), 148-151.

only refute Mr. Holland's thesis but also clarify the dual nature of poetic realism.

Concerning film poetry, Agee desires poetry _of_ the film, instead of poetry _in_ the film. His criticism reveals a consistent acceptance of all types of poetry, as well as a readiness to acknowledge experimental films which attempt to free themselves from photographic realism. Agee's admiration for Laurence Olivier's Henry V is representative: "Above all, his was the whole anti-naturalistic conception of the film -- a true Shakespearean's recognition that man is greater, and nature less, than life" (366). The Battle of Agincourt, which has the "kind of poetic country" Olivier desired, and which is "not realistic," is termed one of the highlights of the film. This kind of interpretation radically differs from the Kracauer advocacy of an accurate photographic rendering of the physical world. Michael Roemer, an adherent of the Kracauer School and director of Nothing But a Man, censures the opening scene of Bergman's Wild Strawberries because the nightmare images, such as a glass coffin and a clock without hands, are "not true film images, derived from life and rendered in concrete, physical terms."[60] Agee never would dismiss summarily any image or experiment for not fitting into a pre-determined class. He judges each film, not for its poundage in physical reality, but for its filmic realization of the original concept.

Agee not only grants that film-makers have the right to work in

[60] "The Surfaces of Reality," Film Quarterly, XVIII (Fall 1964), 15-22.

89

non-realistic modes, but at times applauds such achievements. The

final scene of William Wellman's The Story of G.I. Joe focuses on the
61
dead body of the captain.

> This closing scene seems to me a war poem as
> great and beautiful as any of Whitman's. One
> of the glories of the over-all style and tone
> of the film is its ability to keep itself
> stopped down so low and so lucid, like a partic-
> ularly strong and modest kind of prose, and to
> build a long gently rising arch of increasing
> purity and intensity, which, without a single
> concession to 'poetic' device, culminates in
> the absoluteness of that scene (173).

In addition, the film medium can handle a bewildering, strangely

majestic kind of poetry like Jean Vigo's L'Atalante. The opening

scene of a bridal procession from church to barge, praised but not

described by Agee, is illustrative: the stark white wedding gown,

ill-fitting on an awkwardly shy bride, the accompanying smiling

peasants, the impoverished village streets through which the bride and

groom proudly parade, all contribute to "a great passage, forlorn,

pitiful, cruelly funny, and freezingly sinister" (265).

Numbered among the few great film poems is Farrebique. Agee

believes that this simple one year record of the work and living of a

single farm family, of the farm itself, and the surrounding countryside

conveys "the cold deep-country harshness of Hesiod with a Vergilian

---

61
This is another instance of Agee's critical tendency to be
generous to a fault: The Story of G.I. Joe compares very favorably
with the pulp that passed for fictional war films of the 1940's but it
is not in the same class as Whitman's war poetry or Matthew Brady's
Civil War photographs. This passage, however, documents clearly Agee's
acceptance in theory of poetry of the film.

tenderness and majesty" (299). This film was dismissed at the time
by some critics. Bosley Crowther, for instance, wrote that it contains
no dramatic punch. Agee rejoined that by no means is all of the great
poetry, especially the kind peculiarly suited to the film medium,
dramatic. This nonfiction, undramatic film, pastoral in its tone,
brims with lovely achievements, like Rouquier's treatment of light:

> . . . subdued autumnal light in which the whole
> world is as scratchily distinct as trillions of
> little briars; the veiled shining of spring; the
> supernal light beneath impounded thunder; the
> holy light of snow (299).

Suffused with such poetic sensibility, the film does not suffer from
a lack of dramatic structure. That Agee praises a work for so many
poetic excellences establishes his endorsement of the role of poetry
in the film medium.

Other film theorists, though in the minority, have appreciated the
capacity of the medium to employ poetic modes. Sergei Eisenstein
asserts that the medium is unsurpassed in the use of synecdoche, the
"law of pars pro toto." A close up, because it can isolate one object,
is especially amenable to synecdoche. He also notes the color and
lighting of a shot, as well as the over-all shape of the elements within a frame.[62] A. R. Fulton treats the ability of the medium, in the
words of Willa Cather, to establish "the inexplicable presence of the
thing not named." Though the technique he cites is older than John
Ford's The Informer, the example is appropriate. Gypo, sitting alone
in a pub after receiving money for informing, whispers to himself,

---

[62]
    Film Form and the Film Sense, trans. Jay Leda (Cleveland, 1957),
p. 134.

"I've got to have a plan!" While the camera remains on Gypo, Frankie's voice is heard.

Ah, Gypo, I'm your brain. You can't think without me. [63]
You're lost. You're lost.

Fear, the thing not named, spreads across the screen. Today, these techniques have become part of basic film vocabulary.

Some critics have argued from an aesthetic viewpoint that the inexplicable, or the suggested, is alien to the nature of the medium. Béla Balázs, who twenty years ago anticipated the present Kracauer school, wrote that the film is capable of conveying thoughts and achieving effects through thought, but, "it must not merely suggest them, it must express them explicitly, in film language, of course."[64] The proper province of the film, according to this theory, is the rendering of physical reality, not the creation of an intangible world of suggestion. Hollywood, not for aesthetic but for commercial considerations, has tended over the years to offer its audiences the physical, the direct, and the obvious. Agee points out that the film version of Hemingway's The Killers begins with the author's brilliant, frightening story, but then "spends the next hour or so highlighting all that the story so much more powerfully left in the dark" (217).

In Agee's film esthetic, the indirect has a secure place. As William Empson points out, ambiguity, as long as not intentionally

63
  Fulton, p. 180.

64
  Balázs, p. 129.

sought by the artist, can be satisfying. His claim that "the
strength of vagueness is that it allows of secret ambiguity," is as
applicable to film as to literature.[65]   John Huston handles subtly the
scene in We Were Strangers when, on the steps of Havana's university,
a student is machine-gunned. Immediately hundreds of young men and
women, all in their summer white, fall flat on the steps. The shot
is off the screen before the full meaning is projected: by their
reacting instantly in unison, the students reveal they are used to it
and expect it at any time, and thus this single act is sufficient to
suggest the Cuban tyranny (328-329). Many years before reviewing
this film, Agee excitedly reported in a 1936 letter to Fr. Flye that
he had just discovered Kafka's The Castle, which is "full of terrific
ambiguities and half-lights."[66]   Some sixteen years later, considerably
after Agee's tenure as critic, his television series on Lincoln was
acclaimed particularly because the episodes on Lincoln's death, birth,
and early life had the suggestiveness and lucidity of a parable.[67]   The
classification of Agee as a realist who can only appreciate a
semi-documentary approach is not tenable.

[65]
Seven Types of Ambiguity (New York, 1948), p. 187.

[66]
The Letters of James Agee to Father Flye, ed. Robert Phelps (New
York, 1962), pp. 63-64.

[67]
Meyer Levin, "Abraham Lincoln Through the Picture Tube," The
Reporter, VIII (April 14, 1953), 31-33.

After certain film theorists have pronounced the film unsuited to suggestion, the trend in contemporary cinema is toward ambiguity. Both Pauline Kael and Ivor Montagu deplore what they interpret as the trend of Antonioni and Resnais toward utter vagueness and meaninglessness. Montagu claims that the vague becomes more vague in Antonioni's work, while Alain Resnais has developed "a technique of the portentous so obscure that no one can tell what anything portends."[68] Pauline Kael's pithy judgment on <u>Last Year at Marienbad</u> is that we receive "a snow job in the ice palace," because, after all is over, there is no meaning.[69] Fellini's fluid shifts between objective and subjective reality in $8\frac{1}{2}$ and <u>Juliet of the Spirits</u>, Antonioni's interplay between reality and illusion in <u>Blow-up</u>, Bergman's fusion of two personalities in <u>Persona</u>, Varda's fantasy insets in <u>LeBonheur</u> and $R_e$snais' differentiated consciousness in <u>Muriel</u> are further instances of the film's increasing tendency toward the complex and symbolic, though not necessarily nihilistic. Clearly the burden is now on the film audience, as well as the film critics, to learn to cope with the new, sophisticated film language.[70]

68
Montagu, p. 290.

69
<u>I Lost It At the Movies</u> (New York, 1966), p. 167.

70
Amos Vogel, "The Onus Is Not on the Artist; It is We Who Must Learn," <u>The New York Times</u> (September, 1966), p.D15.

Stanley Kubrick's ending to 2001: A Space Odyssey has proven burden-
some to audiences. Jarring juxtapositions, like a spacecraft parked
inside a bedroom, occur during sudden shifts of time and action as the
protagonist sees himself, projected for the first instant as someone
else in another location, at successively older stages in his life.
This final sequence is purely visual, with no concessions to verbal
explanations over the soundtrack. Although it runs the risk of
confusing, to the point of irritating, some moviegoers, I am certain
Agee would warmly endorse this film as most finely representative of
the newer direction of the cinema in the late 1960's.

Agee, in dealing with the few films in the 1940's which seriously
attempted symbolism or allegory, applies standards consistent with his
belief in realism. The unreal in any form has to be founded on solid
reality. Without a context of plausibility, film symbolism or allegory
becomes one-dimensional. John Ford's adaptation of The Power and the
Glory, The Fugitive, turns Graham Greene's protagonist into a
"creeping Jesus."

> I doubt that Jesus ever crept, and I am sickened
> when I watch others creep in His name; I dislike
> allegory and symbolism which are imposed on and
> denature reality as deeply as I love both when
> they bloom from and exalt reality (289).

Another film which tempers the reality to fit the allegory is
Hitchcock's Lifeboat, the story of a derelict boat and its passengers.
Although the film is at times fascinating as a technical tour de force,
the allegory is too well worked out, "too carefully slide-ruled." It
does not give off "the crazy, more than ambiguous, nascent oxygen
quality of first-rate allegories like those of Shakespeare or Kafka

or Joyce;" by this explanation (more poetic than scientific) Agee
suggests the exhilarating effect from contact with the indefinable (72).

In these negative reviews of films attempting complex symbolism
or allegory, there is no hint of any inherent incapacity of the film
medium. The fault is with the film-makers.

The same criterion is applied to fantasy as to allegory. The
supernatural must be treated as natural. Salvador Dali's dream
sequence in Hitchcock's Spellbound fails because it is irrelevant to
dream reality and lacks any discernible connection with reality (180).
In another film, Another Time Around, Agee notes that the element of
magic is engaging, but it progressively loses appeal as there is not
enough sense of real life by which to measure its wonder.[71]

This call for realism, even in the midst of fantasy, is different
from the theory of photographic realism, now dominant in film criticism.
Although both Agee and Kracauer, the major proponent of the other
school, demand the illusion of reality in the film, there is a
fundamental distinction. Kracauer believes that the only valid way to
treat fantasy is lightly and playfully, or else the "camera reality"
will be violated.[72] Agee would dismiss this concept as extreme. David
Lean's version of Great Expectations has shortcomings, but its blend of
fantasy and realism succeeds, because Lean realizes that "a dream must
be presented, even at its weirdest moments, matter of factly and on
its own terms."[73] This judgment is similar to Agee's admiration for the

[71]"Another Time Around," Time, L (September 29, 1947), 98-103.

[72]Theory of Film, p. 187.

[73]"Great Expectations," Time, XLIX (May 26, 1947), 99-102.

novel Descent Into Hell. Charles Williams takes the supernatural for granted, without distrust or doubt; and without any overtones of agnosticism or atheism.[74]   Such an attitude assures the framework of credibility, not playfulness, Agee considers vital to the presentation of supernatural fiction.

Alexander Dovzhenko, an original film poet, injects the fantastic freely and frankly into his politically fervent Arsenal. This experimental piece, with talking horses, portraits that come to life, and bullet-proof Bolsheviks, is set within a framework of reality. Released in 1929 shortly after Trotsky was expelled from the Soviet Union, it seriously and simply narrates the tragedy of a defeat.[75] Not conforming in the least to Kracauer's dictum, this film is an historical example of Agee's position.

Agee's script for The African Queen was hailed by the critics as lively adventure with a touch of fantasy.[76]   Consistent with his critical theory, Agee maintains a degree of plausibility in the characters, and thereby assures a basis of realism in the film. The differences between C. S. Forester, author of the novel, and Agee in the treatment of characters is pronounced. Most notably, the characters of Rose and Allunt are transformed by Agee: Rose from a

---

[74] The Letters of James Agee to Father Flye, p. 186. In literature, this principle of verisimilitude has been well and long established, as in Swift's Gulliver's Travels.

[75] George A. Huaco, The Sociology of Film Art (New York,1965), p. 124.

[76] Oakley, p. 215.

one-dimensional, patriotic British old maid to a fiery, very feminine
force to be reckoned with; Allnutt from an immature, dependent Cockney
forever "cooing" to a virile, independent, but driftless skipper.
Although Katherine Hepburn's and Humphrey Bogart's personalities
reinforce the types of transformed characters in the film, these
differences are discernible from an examination of the script and
novel by themselves.

A passage from Let Us Now Praise Famous Men supplies further
evidence of Agee's opposition to extreme realism, which, in effect,
patronizes fantasy by insisting on its always being treated lightly.

> Without any qualification and if necessary with
> belligerence I respect and believe in even the
> most supposedly 'fantastic' works of the imagin-
> ation. I am indeed ready to say, because with
> fair consistence I believe, that works of the
> imagination (chiefly because in a certain degree
> they create something which has never existed
> before, they add to and somewhat clarify the sum
> total of the state of being whereas the rest of
> the mind's activity is merely deductive, descrip-
> tive, acquisitive or contemplative), advance and
> assist the human race, and make an opening in the
> darkness around it, as nothing else can.[77]

Through the haze of this type of youthful, evangelical writing, Agee
cautions that imaginative works are double-edged: as they can liberate
and enlighten, so they can distort and corrupt. In the same sense, an
over-reliance on documentary realism can destroy any sense of reality.
In Agee's judgment, it is a mutually respectful, enriching union
between poetry and realism that is most suited to the film.

77
Let Us Now Praise Famous Men, p. 232.

Agee believes that motion and a visual quality are essential for the medium to realize its fullest potential.[78]   In the review of DeMille's The Crusades, he enumerates its glaring faults, but concludes that DeMille undeniably has a film sense, since his works are "masterly affirmations of cinema's first law: keep it moving."[79] Yet Agee does not subscribe to motion for motion's sake. He commends Michael Curtiz, director of Casablanca, for having the director's correct feeling, epitomized in the American films of the twenties, that everything, including the camera, should move. However, "the camera should move for purposes other than those of a nautch-dancer" (29). One of the masters in Hollywood of montage, Slavko Vorkapich, writes that although he interjected wordless sequences of "motion" into countless films (the opening frames of Crime Without Passion), he rejects the idea that motion is magic. Too many directors use dolly and boom shots simply to infuse massive doses of motion into a film. Vorkapich maintains, as Agee does, that there has to be a reason for each movement, arising out of the subject matter.[80]

---

[78]
These distinctions, which in fact do not exist, since what is in motion or seen may also be real and/or poetic, are made only for the purpose of close analysis in this chapter.

[79]
"Also Showing," Time, LI (June 7, 1948), 98-102.

[80]
Ezra Goodman, The Fifty Year Decline and Fall of Hollywood (New York, 1962), p. 294.

Although motion is not a sine qua non, its absence, for most films, is too great an obstacle to overcome. Even the film artist Sergei Eisenstein in _Ivan the Terrible, Part I_ is not entirely able to avoid the enervating effects of a lack of motion, although many of his massive stills are sculpturally impressive. Yet the over-all result of Eisenstein's experimentally abandoning significant, sustained movement is that his peculiar energy becomes, according to Agee, "cold, musclebound, and sombre" (248). This particular critical failure is not meant to serve categorically for all films. On occasions, there have been admirable films with no appreciable motion, like Zoltan Korda's static version of _The Macomber Affair_, which is so daringly ascetic in its demands of all the film is supposed to need most and do best that only a few directors have tried it, and even fewer have succeeded.[81]

Carl Dreyer has persistently violated most of the "rules" of cinema, principally the one concerning motion. Though granting that Dreyer is far out at the edge, rather than close to the center of all that might be most productive and original, Agee honors him as a film artist. _Day of Wrath_ receives qualified, though appreciative, recognition for creating motion portraits rather than drama. Dreyer, nevertheless, is able to fashion "grave and noble drama of his portraits."[82] Agee is willing to admit that Dreyer should be credited

[81] "The New Pictures," _Time_, XLV (April 30, 1947), 89-91.

[82] "The New Pictures," _Time_, LI (May 24, 1948), 96-100.

with mastering the technique of motionlessness.[83] Most other critics

have tended to reject Dreyer's work as being too ponderous, heavy and

slow. Richard Schickel, with characteristic critical myopia, charges

that Joan of Arc and Day of Wrath are intolerable in the stateliness

of their pace and their agonizing lingering over detail.[84]

Agee rejects such critical syllogisms: all films must have

motion; this film does not have sufficient motion; therefore this

film fails. He would agree with Rene Clair's statement that if there

is an aesthetics of the cinema, "it could be summarized in one word:

Movement."[85] After agreeing, he would then applaud unhesitatingly

films like The Macomber Affair and Day of Wrath, which are essentially

static, not partaking of any substantial physical, spatial, or camera

motion. Only a work of art integrates all of the diverse elements of

the film. Many minor masterpieces excel in one area. A coordination

of motion, image, sound, and meaning, in a visually oriented film,

informed by poetic realism, constitutes the supreme filmic achievement

in Agee's terms.

These are the criteria applied in judging a film, not a dogmatic

insistence on "motion." George Bluestone, in contrast, argues that

---

[83]
Since Agee's day, the remarkable Dreyer has not changed. His last
film, Gertrud (1964), again violates fundamental rules: it is extremely
slow moving and relies primarily on words. Comparable to Stravinsky's
The Rite of Spring, it caused an uproar of disapproval at its premiere
in Paris.

[84]
Movies, the History of an Art and an Institution,(New York,1964)p.76.

[85]
Edward Wagenknecht, The Movies in the Age of Innocence (Oklahoma,
1962), p. 21.

movement is the pivotal element in film structure, because the conflict of individuals or groups projected on the screen is, unlike that of any other medium's story structure, in constant motion.[86] This type of distinction seems clever, but actually is irrelevant. Any good conflict, whether seen on a stage or read in a novel, will contain inherent tension and motion. Of highest priority to Agee are whether the motion in a film is meaningful; the characters plausible; the theme realized. In short, motion is fundamental, not indispensable.

The visual power of the medium was eloquently described by President Woodrow Wilson, who, after a private showing of The Birth of a Nation at the White House, exclaimed that it is like writing history in flashes of lightning. Agee is no exception to the consensus of film theorists and laymen that all elements in a film should communicate primarily and directly to the eyes. This visual dimension, in contrast to motion, is a sine qua non of the film. There are no corresponding Carl Dreyers who have successfully negated the visual orientation of the medium. Agee unequivocally states that there is only one rule for films he finally cares about, "that the film interest the eyes, and do its job through the eyes" (305). The essential idiom of the film is "the visual telling of stories" (330).

The Russian directors of the 1920's demanded the same visual consciousness. V. I. Pudovkin writes of the need for "expressive plastic material," and believes that a director's task is to select from the unlimited supply of life those visual images which require

---

86
Bluestone, p. 52.

no explanation, and yet carry a clear and definite meaning.[87]   Sergei

Eisenstein acknowledges the all-pervasive influence of the visual by

citing a problem he encountered during the filming of <u>Alexander Nevsky</u>.

He could not convey to Prokofiev, the musical composer for the film,

a sense of the music he desired for a battle scene. Finally,

Eisenstein ordered some prop instruments constructed, shot them being

played visually without sound, and projected the results. Prokofiev

immediately knew what effect Eisenstein wanted "seen" in the music,

and shortly after gave him the musical equivalent of the visual

projection.[88]   Eisenstein with validity uses this incident to

substantiate the claim that all elements of the film are deeply visual.

In Agee's estimation, Hollywood in the 1940's was responsible for

a vast output of visually sterile, word-dominated films, like the

M.G.M. production of Saroyan's <u>The Human Comedy</u>.

> In the closing sequence a young man, an orphan,
> arrives who has never seen the town before and
> has heard much of it. He wants to look at it,
> tenderly and at leisure. He might have been
> the vehicle for as fine a summation as an
> American town could ever get. What does the
> camera do instead? Close-ups of his face, while
> his stream of consciousness murmurs that there
> is the library, and the Presbyterian Church,
> and so on. (32-33).

The Italian neo-realists, during the same period, endowed their

films with visual life. Vittorio da Sica's <u>Shoeshine</u> contains nothing

tricky, "arty," or visually fancy. Nor is it cinematically original,

---

[87]
Pudovkin, p. 58.

[88]
<u>Film Form and the Film Sense</u>, trans. Jay Leda (Cleveland, 1957)
p. 159.

like the work of Jean Vigo. Yet, it depicts the way that places and

things and people look, act, and inter-act, and abundantly conveys

this information to the eye.[89] This last line serves as a concise,

rudimentary definition of what Agee means by the visual: having

something to say, and saying it to the eyes.

Movies should tell their stories more for the eyes than the ears.[90]

The essay Agee wrote for the Harlem photographs of Helen Levitt,

collected in A Way of Seeing, explains his rationale for emphasizing

the visual. The mind and spirit of man are formed by, and in turn

inform, the senses: "The busiest and most abundant of the senses is

that of sight."[91] Ernest Lindgren corroborates this theory by

arguing that sight is the most important of our senses, since we know

and learn far more from the world around us through our eyes than

through our ears. Because of this, the visual part of a sound film

carries more of the total significance.[92] John Ford, who became

established as a director of silent films, has adapted well to the

changed medium of the sound film, precisely because he continues to

[89] "Shoeshine," Time, L (September 8, 1947), 99-100.

[90] "Ivy," Time, L (July 7, 1947), 66-68. Always flexible, Agee admitted exceptions: Hamlet is praised because Olivier decided to make the poetry primary.

[91] A Way of Seeing, p. 3.

[92] The Art of the Film (New York, 1963), p. 104.

emphasize the visual. Agee, Lindgren, and the other film theorists who argue that sight should predominate over sound would support John Ford's practical guideline, "I believe the movies are primarily pictures, so I play them that way."[93]

There has not been unanimous critical agreement on the role of the visual. One school, typified by the film critics of the 1930's, maintains that the sound of a film is only one element which helps to complete the picture, just as any shadow or line. Words should be decidedly subordinate and, above all, weightless.[94] I am certain Agee would reject this theory. He is too concerned with the meaning of a film, in part conveyed by the dialogue, to relegate sound to the level of a shadow or a compositional line in a particular frame. D. W. Griffith is another proponent of an almost exclusive role for the visual. A month before his death in 1947, he charged that the modern film has "taken beauty and exchanged it for stilted voices." Griffith felt that there has been too much dependence on the voice, and that the film should concentrate on the visual beauty in the world: "the beauty of moving wind in the trees, the little movement in a beautiful blowing on the blossoms in the trees."[95] To Agee, a film is great only if it is imbued with significance. It is not enough, contrary to Griffith and theorists like Béla Balázs and Siegfried Kracauer, to

---

[93]
   Quoted but not identified in Fulton, p. 172.

[94]
   Balázs, p. 229.

[95]
   Quoted in Goodman, p. 19.

record ripples in a pond, trees moving in the wind, or an oncoming
train.

Agee advocates a primary, not exclusive, role for the visual.
Eisenstein's Ivan the Terrible, though interesting as an oddly creative,
bold undertaking, nevertheless is censured for only partially fulfilling
the visual function of a film: it speaks to the eyes, but has little
to say.[96]

> The picture is splendid to look at; yet there is
> little that is superior to, or much different
> from, the Russian operatic and theatrical
> mannerisms which must have been over-rich and
> over-digested a generation ago (249).

Similarly, the war documentary Listen to Britain proves dull, even
though the sights predominate, because they are commonplace.[97] Although
the eye is the most receptive of the senses, and the visual
indispensable to the medium, Agee demands more than a parading of
vacuous sights.

The history of the film contains a glaring example of an
inordinate emphasis on the visual. German Expressionism of the 1920's
crowded out story line, characterization, and theme for the sake of
visual realization. Masses of people were organized architecturally,
and the individual human figure was subordinated to the composition of
large objects. A subjective camera technique, as well as camera

---

[96]
Agee's judgment must be taken in context: compared to Eisenstein's
earlier films, in which ideas are as abundant as his newly-found visual
poetry, Ivan the Terrible has little to say; compared to the bulk of
movies distributed, it has a great deal to say.

[97]
"Documentaries Grow Up," Time XLII, (September 13, 1943), 94-95.

mobility, dominated. In time, all subtitles were eliminated.[98] This experiment, in almost exclusively focusing on the visual, did produce some startling films, like Robert Wiene's The Cabinet of Dr. Caligari and Fritz Lang's Metropolis. The entire movement, however, proved suicidally short-lived. In contrast to this radical development is the trend in the 1960's. Meaning, significance, and theme, although at times disturbingly vague, are present. Amos Vogel, director of the Lincoln Center Film Festival, discerns a thrust towards "a freer, more poetic, visually oriented cinema," but one with meaning.[99] Agee, who urged such a development twenty years ago, would endorse this emphatic, meaningful role of the visual.

Although Agee's film scripts reveal a practical grasp of the possibilities in the medium, his fiction demonstrates a decidedly visual awareness, particularly the posthumously published A Death in the Family. Much of the novel's prose is projected in a camera-like panning and focusing on one object at a time. As Rufus approaches his father's coffin during the wake, he sees in detail the appearance of the coffin at different distances, in the manner of the classic camera set-ups of long shot, medium, and close-up:

> 'Come, now,' their mother whispered, and, taking
> them each by the hand, led him through the Green
> Room and into the living room.
>   There it was against the fireplace, and there
> seemed to be scarcely anything else in the room
> except the sunny light on the floor.
>   It was very long and dark; smooth like a boat;

98
    Huaco, pp. 14-16.

99"The Onus is Not on the Artist; It Is We Who Must Learn!" New York Times, September 11, 1966, p. D15.

with bright handles. Half the top was open . . . .
There was his head, his arms; suit: there he
was. . . . The arm was bent. Out of the dark
suit, the starched cuff, sprang the hairy wrist.
The wrist was angled; the hand was arched;
none of the fingers touched each other.
The hand was so composed that it seemed at
once casual and majestic. It stood exactly above
the center of his body.
The fingers looked unusually clean and dry,
as if they had been scrubbed with great care.
The hand looked very strong, and the veins
were strong in it.

After mention of the arm, Agee proceeds successively with close-ups of

the wrist, hand, and fingers. This lingering over detail serves to

convey Rufus' mute amazement at all of the strange facts about his

strangely indifferent father. Agee possessed, as Leslie Fiedler

accurately expresses it, the rare gift of seeing the world in "sharp,

fragmented sights -- all detailed foregrounds." [100]

The film scripts, on the other hand, contain concrete instructions

which testify to Agee's appreciation of the visual nature of the medium,

yet they are not the original, detailed treatments one would expect

from such a poetic, visually oriented writer. Noa-Noa, never produced,

strives for some exotic visual effects, like the parallel between

Gauguin's death and his painting of "The Yellow Christ." At the

instant of Gaugin's death, the camera holds on Christ as honey seeps

from his body. [101] The surest visual achievement in all five scripts

occurs in the opening scene of The African Queen. Agee devised a church

---

[100]
"Encounter with Death," New Republic, CXXXVI (December 9, 1957),
25-26.

[101]
Agee on Film, Vol. II: Five Film Scripts, pp. 146-47.

service, not in C. S. Forester's novel, to provide insights into the characters of Allnutt, Rose, and Samuel. Whereas Forester reports the personalities of his characters, Agee shows them. Rose, for instance, though indubitably the British gentlewoman by her apparel, demeanor, and position, is portrayed in the opening scene as inured to jungle life. While playing the organ at the opening church service, an "exotic and horrible centipede-like creature" slithers into view between two organ keys. Rose, without interrupting her playing, nonchalantly brushes it away. In this way, Agee introduces, without dialogue, Rose's British pluckiness, which later provides much of the humor as Allnutt and she bungle their way down the river on The 102 African Queen.

Throughout Agee's criticism, emphasis on the visual never suggests that it is sufficient by itself. It is only one, though a potent, component of the medium; if completely unchecked, it can overwhelm the whole. In the same way, motion is included in the preferred film style, not in deference to any intrinsic superiority of physical movement, but because of the natural flow of the medium. For Agee, no one element is a panacea. Only in a creative convergence of the visual, motion, poetry, and realism will the film achieve its most fecund style.

102
Agee on Film, Vol. II: Five Film Scripts, p. 152. This bit of business was short-sightedly cut from the final film version, by director John Huston or one of his editors. In any case, it remains an adroit piece of visual characterization.

CHAPTER III

THE TECHNIQUES OF THE FILM

Father Flye recently recalled Agee's youthful attachment to the
movies, and, particularly, his fascination with the capacities of a
camera. He would be excited about the action and adventure of a film,
like most boys of thirteen or fourteen, but also would be interested
in the camera placements and angles, the tracking or panning shots, and
the degree of control the director exercised over the camera.[1] The
criticism and film scripts testify that his interest proved to be a
lifelong involvement. This chapter examines Agee's attention to the
technical side of movie-making, since it comprises a significant part
of the film esthetic.[2]

Throughout the reviews, Agee calls attention to the recording
power of the camera. About the documentary "Hymn of Nations," he writes
that the camera's retention on the sensitive face of conductor Arturo
Toscanini produces "as good a record of human existence somewhere near

---

[1]
    This information was obtained during an interview with Father
Flye on January 9, 1968, in New York City.

[2]
    To date there has been no study in print of this part of Agee's
criticism. I find this surprising in light of the general awakening
of interest in film techniques, and the focus on Agee as a film critic,
both of which have occurred during the past few years.

its utmost" as it is possible to obtain.[3] In this instance, the camera records with fidelity a profoundly human experience, an artist deeply involved in his work. In a war documentary, "To the Shores of Iwo Jima," there is "a closeup of a bullet-hole in flesh, at once as intimate and as impersonal as if it were your own wound, so new you cannot feel it."[4] No words are used or needed. The camera, by recording this type of detail, enables communication without the aid of verbal commentary.

Years before his first film review, Agee referred to this recording capacity of the camera. If operated straightforwardly, without any manipulation by the operator, it is "incapable of recording anything but absolute, dry truth."[5] Twelve years later, a more experienced Agee believed this only conditionally, placing greater emphasis on the indeterminate factor, the operator of the camera. It is clear, he wrote in A Way of Seeing, that "the camera never lies" is a foolish saying. Most people, however, probably do not know just how "extraordinarily slippery a liar the camera is." It is a scientific instrument which records with impressive fidelity what is in the eye, mind, spirit, and skill of its operator to make it record. "It is, in

---

[3] James Agee, Agee on Film: Reviews and Comments (New York, 1958), p. 200. All further references, which will be set in parentheses in the text, are to this edition.

[4] "To the Shores of Iwo Jima," Time, XLV (March 26, 1945), 91-96. Unsigned review by Agee.

[5] Let Us Now Praise Famous Men (Boston, 1960), p. 254.

fact, hard to get the camera to tell the truth; yet it can be made to, in many ways and on many levels."[6] This view, contrasted with the earlier one, represents a more balanced, mature understanding.

Many contemporary film-makers have stressed the potential of the camera. A former painter, now a film-maker, James E. Davis, sees it as an instrument which permits the artist to communicate all that is new and progressive in contemporary existence. For the first time in history, the artist can express reality dynamically instead of statically. He can depict concepts of modern science and philosophy that had defied representation: The Bergsonian flux of time, the continuous process of becoming, the relativism implicit in the space-time concept, time as the fourth dimension, and the space-time continuum. These processes, altering our thoughts and dreams, can now be approached through the motion picture camera.[7] While in basic agreement with the concepts, Agee would not endorse the sweeping manner in which Davis makes these claims. Ingmar Bergman pays tribute to the camera more simply and directly by declaring that a director performs conjuring tricks with apparatus so expensive and so wonderful that any entertainer in history would have given anything to have it.[8] He calls the camera "the most precious and the most astouding magical

[6] A Way of Seeing (New York, 1965), p. 3.

[7] James E. Davis, "The Only Dynamic Art," in Introduction to the Art of the Movies, ed. Lewis Jacobs (New York, 1960), pp. 277-278.

[8] Four Screenplays of Ingmar Bergman (New York, 1960), p. xv.

device" that has ever, since history began, been put into the hands
of an artist.[9] Not only feats of magic, Bergman's films penetrate
man's spiritual crises.

Specifically, the camera derives much of its power from the single
shot and the close-up. Agee views the latter primarily as a means for
intensifying effect. Eisenstein's daring use of the close-up charges
his films with intimacy and immediacy. In Ivan the Terrible, the
"Shakespearean intensity of the great static close-ups" is
remarkable.[10] As Eisenstein's chief device in this work, the many
close-ups enhance the anti-naturalistic, superhuman effect (370).
Conversely, close-ups can help to create realism in a film. John
Huston's use of the unexpected close-up of Edward G. Robinson soaking
in a bathtub in Key Largo "reverberates like a gong," because of its
sudden impact. It also provides for one of the most memorable first
entrances of a character on record (328). V. I. Pudovkin, for the
same reason but with bombast, extolls the close-up as "the keystone
of the whole power and effectiveness of the cinema," since it
eliminates the supererogatory.[11] By keeping everything out of the frame
except the one object or action of significance to be viewed, the
close-up can directly penetrate to the core of a scene. By a close-up

[9] Film Makers on Film Making, ed. Harry M. Geduld (Bloomington, 1967), pp. 178-179.

[10] "Boos and Bravos," Time, VLVII (April 1, 1946), 93-96.

[11] Film Technique and Film Acting (New York, 1960), p. 218.

on parched corn served to Confederate troops in trenches at the close
of the Civil War, D. W. Griffith, in The Birth of a Nation, suggested
the frayed glory of the South.

Agee is conscious that the close-up can effect a bodily
kinesthetic change in the viewer. In a sudden cut from a long view
of an object to a very close view, there is an inevitable optical and
kinesthetic impact, an explosive magnification, a sudden leap forward.
The director then decides the degrees of change, impact, and intensity
appropriate for a particular scene. Agee's script for The African
Queen contains a few instances of the close-up used for manipulating
emotional tones. Rose, early in the film, resorts to the silent
treatment to force Allnutt into agreeing with her patriotic,
dangerous scheme of navigating down a river to blow up a German patrol
vessel.

    Allnut. And you call yourself a Christian. (Silence)
        You 'ear me, Miss. (Silence). Don't yer?
        (Silence; a bright cruel idea. Louder, leaning
        to her.) Don't yer? (Silence. Suddenly, at
        the top of his lungs.) HUH??

    EXTREME CLOSE-UP ROSE
        (In spite of herself she flinches; but swiftly
        controls it.)

    LONG SHOT - FROM OTHER SIDE OF THE RIVER
        A half mile of hot, empty water, then jungle,
        silent on a dream of heat. On the far side
        the tiny boat and the two infinitesimal
        passengers.

        After two seconds, Allnutt's 'HUH?' is heard

    EXTREME CLOSE-UP - ROSE
        In her face are victory, cruelty, and tremendous
        secret gratification: a Jocasta digesting her
        young.

The ECHO comes. Over it-)

CUT TO

12

EXTREME CLOSE-UP - ALLNUTT

The jarring use of alternating close-ups and long shots produces
sensations of kinesthetic, optical displacements to parallel the
emotional battering of Allnutt.

The camera's capacity to project a striking single shot, a basic
part of film grammar, has been used by film-makers principally to
effect a heightened emotional impact. To have full power, an image
must be introduced and given its own pure existence for a few seconds
without any sound, music, explanation, or comment. In the word
dominated movies of the 1940's, images were often dissipated by music
and commentary, supplied, it seemed, by the Mormom Tabernacle Choir
and the Voice of God (164).

On the other hand, no director, in Agee's judgment, has
surpassed Sergei Eisenstein in understanding and fully exploiting
the power of the single shot. A smashed eyeglass over the bloodied
eye of a woman in Potemkin, the architectually poised battle lines
in Alexander Nevsky, and the coronation scene in Ivan the Terrible
reveal Eisenstein's method of intensifying impact. In the latter
scene, Agee notes two shots in particular: the deacon during his
hair-raising intonation of the royal benediction, and the tumescent
face of the new Czar while gold coins are ritualistically poured over

---

12
   Agee on Film, Vol. II: Five Film Scripts (New York, 1960),
pp. 205-206.

him (250). Without explaining the theory involved, Agee often singles
out the great shots in a film. The single shot produces intensity by
two means. Because it is startling, it seems to leap out at the
viewer, bringing about a kinesthetic, optical reaction analogous
to the effect of the close-up. The single shot also seems to stop
all motion, blurring in the eye of the viewer the succeeding and
preceding frames. Movement appears arrested so that the one striking
shot can settle.

Emphasizing single shots is one of the many ways in which a
director takes active charge of the camera. When employed skillfully,
the camera becomes a brush to produce visual images, impressions,
shadings, and nuances of meaning. Elia Kazan achieves such effects
in A Tree Grows in Brooklyn:

> There is a shot of the girl hesitant on a curb
> which has the lovely authenticity of a wild
> animal startled by a flashbulb -- or of the
> same shot made by a concealed camera in a real
> street. There is a shot of Dunn, ghastly drunk
> in his inky waiter's suit, so painfully
> malappropriate[sic] to daylight, being shoved
> and shouted along his home street, which is
> as poetic and individualized an image of a state
> beneath humiliation as I have seen (142).

Agee sharply distinguishes between an active and passive use of
the camera. Both styles have possibilities as well as limitations.
A director must decide which type is more appropriate for a particular
film. The active camera takes its story "by the scruff of the neck"
and tells it, while the passive camera is transparent, simply
receiving and purely recording what is in front of it (329). Though
Agee accepts the active camera as a fundamental of film grammar, there

are, regrettably, only scattered examples of its effective use: in
the Western The Lady Takes a Chance, scrambled focus conveys
excitement and intoxication; [13] in Farrebique, slow motion shows the
motions of darkness, light, and shadow, and captures the bursting out
and blossoming of the world in spring (298).

In sundry reviews, Agee cites three directors, in the history of
the film, as masters of the active camera. D. W. Griffith, the
manipulator of so many other cinematic techniques, generously injects
his personality into his films by means of a camera. His images are
generally a little larger and wilder than life; his frame is always
full, spontaneous, and lively (316). This appraisal is accurate, but
Agee offers no specific examples. He could have referred to the scene
in Broken Blossoms when Chang Huon and Lucy first look at each other,
she in the street and he in the shop. The audience looks through the
eyes of each, first seeing the girl as the man sees her, and then the
objects in the shop as they appear to Lucy's delighted gaze. [14] Jean
Vigo and Alfred Hitchcock similarly thrust the camera's eye into the
thick of the action. "Zero de Conduite" evidences Vigo's sure hand:
the subtly slurred rather than slow motion; the dormitory riot which
culminates in a slow motion storm of pillow feathers. Vigo, like
Griffith, is not afraid to experiment with a "subjective," or active

_____

[13]
"The New Pictures," Time, XLII (September 20, 1943), 94-96.

[14]
Edward Wagenknecht, The Movies in the Age of Innocence (Oklahoma,
1962), p. 121, includes in his work an essay on Griffith which is both
reminiscent and perceptive.

camera. The camera becomes one of the characters. Although the device
is somewhat difficult to grasp immediately, Vigo portrays the school
children as they see and are seen by each other (263). This provides
various perspectives of the characters.

Agee terms Alfred Hitchcock one of the few living men who knows
just when and how to use the active (subjective) camera. In
Spellbound (1949) some of the "unlimited, cryptic terror which can
reside in mere objects" is captured when the patient enters the
bathroom and the camera hesitatingly scans the room (180). The
character's increasing anxiety and mental imbalance are thus
projected. Hitchcock's dexterity with an active camera has been
clearly evidenced in the two decades since Agee's time, through Jimmy
Stewart's helplessness in Rear Window, Stewart's dizziness in Vertigo,
Janet Leigh's horror in Psycho, and Cary Grant's confusion in North
by Northwest.

This type of inventive camera work was rare during the 1940's.
Although Wellman's The Story of G.I. Joe is termed a masterpiece, Agee
feels compelled to add, "I still wonder what might have been done if
during one combat sequence the camera had worked inside some
individual as well as outside" (174). A. R. Fulton, in the same
manner, argues for the effectiveness of the subjective camera in
contrast to the objective or passive. For evidence, he cites two
scenes in the film version of William Inge's Picnic. The opening
frames reveal a train rushing straight at the camera. Shortly after,
the hero explores the town into which the train has brought him. As
he crosses a backyard and approaches a house, the camera is behind

him so that the viewer, in approaching with the hero, can identify
with his hesitancy and apprehension. What makes the commonplace
backyard scene more exciting than the spectacular train scene is the
subjective point of view.[15]   Like Picnic, the films of the 1960's
seem to be tending toward a more camera-oriented, cinematic, rather
than literary, style. Jonas Mekas, prophet of The Village Voice,
proclaims the death of the "old cinema," which he labels nothing
more than an extension of the theatre. The new cinema, though
retaining narration, will concentrate on image and movement composed
by film poets. Mekas intones, with Old Testament inflection, "the
light of this new art is bursting on the world like a new dawn."
Many of the newer, more experimental film-makers have agreed with
Mekas that what matters is not the story a film tells, but the image
on the screen. To vary and vitalize the succession of images, they
tilt the camera, turn it upside down, jiggle it, and wave it around.[16]

Agee would dismiss this movement. Even though he believes that
fertile, unrealized possibilities exist in the active use of the
camera, he warns of its dominance or intrusion. He condemns in one
film the freeze frames and accelerated shots as "camera tricks,"

---

[15]
Motion Pictures (Oklahoma, 1960), p. 273.

[16]
"Art of Light and Lunacy: The New Underground Films," Time,
February 17, 1967, pp. 94-95. These camera hi-jinks have even
penetrated, in the experimentalist's jargon, Hollywood's "plastic
bag," with such a groovy commercial production as Roger Corman's
The Trip (1967).

over-frequent and over-affected.[17] In contrast is Rouquier's pure
treatment of man and nature in Farrebique, in which there is no
elaborate composing, no fancy work with filters or soft focus, no
picturesqueness. The camera accepts and sensitively records the more
than sufficient beauty of the world.[18] As with motion in the film,
Agee does not favor strong camera activity for its own sake. He
praises the documentary Desert Victory for allowing the camera to
record unobtrusively. It does not reveal a brilliant, creative
collaboration of cameras, but neither is there a shot which dishonors
its subject by any sort of affectation, sentimentality, or contrivance.
The passive camera provides an opportunity for conveying the
"magnificence which any face or machine or light or terrain possesses,
left to its own devices" (33). There is, simply, an abundance to
behold in the world as it can be recorded by the camera.

A significant number of film theorists have differed with Agee's
acceptance of the passive camera. Edward Fischer charges that Twelve
Angry Men, a Sidney Lumet film in which the camera seldom leaves the
jury room, is comparable in effect to hearing a symphony orchestra
play at half-strength. An orchestra can play, even well, with only
half of its instruments, but it is capable of doing far more. Fischer
then gives as an example of a fully orchestrated film David Lean's

[17]
"How to Finance a Movie," Time, LI (April 19, 1948), 100-104.

[18]
"Farrebique," Time, LI (March 15, 1948), 100-104.

The Bridge on the River Kwai, in which the camera is liberated.[19]
Agee would evaluate films from a broader base. One film would not be
judged better than another on the basis of camera activity. A succinct
statement of his viewpoint is made in a defiant defense of Monsieur
Verdoux. He upholds Chaplin for believing that "if you can invent
something worth watching, the camera should hold still and clear, so
you can watch it. That is still, and will always be, one of the best
possible ways to use a camera" (255). This principle, enunciated in
1947, differs from the foregoing quotation concerning the 1943 Desert
Victory. In 1943, Agee was in the earlier part of his career as film
critic, and still under the influence of his anti-art thesis, pro-
pounded in Let Us Now Praise Famous Men. In 1947, after four years of
reviewing films, he added a significant qualification for the passive
camera. There must be something worth watching, and not just, as
stated in the earlier quotation, any face, machine, light, or terrain.

Jean Cocteau attempted to maintain a strictly passive camera in
the filming of The Beauty and the Beast (1947). He declared in the
beginning of his diary that, in a spirit of instinctive contradiction,
all camera movement would be avoided. At that time, camera activity
was so much in fashion that the experts thought it indispensable.
Cocteau set out to prove them wrong.[20] For the sedan-chair scene, a
long tracking shot was used, but later deleted so that the film would

19
The Screen Arts (New York, 1960), p. 45.

20
Diary of a Film (New York, 1950), p. 27.

prove it possible to avoid all camera movement and keep to a fixed
frame.[21] Agee, a rebel himself, would admire Cocteau's spirit, but
would deem the experiment needless. Why intentionally deny this
scientific instrument its full range? As he opposes camera tricks, so
would he oppose camera rigidity. In Noa-Noa, there are directions
for dolly and tracking shots, stop shots, shifts from color to black
and white, and subjective camera uses.[22] Agee's experience with
photographer Walker Evans taught him that the camera can be much more
than a mere recorder of the actual. In the hands of an artist, it
can be an interpreter and maker of metaphor.[23]

In Agee's judgment, the subject matter of the film is diverse
enough to permit a full range of camera use, as demonstrated in the
work of Chaplin, Griffith, Vigo, and Hitchcock. He does not argue
exclusively for either the active or passive camera. The use of a
camera should be dictated by the non-technical dimensions of plot,
character, setting, and theme of a particular work. However potent

---

21
Cocteau, p. 50.

22
One of these subjective camera uses consists in placing the camera
in a coffin. Mourners at a funeral come to pay their last respects
and look directly into the lens. David Lean effectively used a
similar device, some twelve years later, in his version of Doctor
Zhivago.

23
Gerald Weales, "The Critic in Love," Reporter, XIX (December 25,
1958), 38-39, examines some of the implications in the relationship
between Agee and Walker Evans.

its capacity, the camera has a supplementary role.

A nagging belief in the recording power of the camera is demonstrated by Agee's demand for actual locations. He calls for their use not for any mystical reason, but on the premise that real environments can exert a creative influence on all connected with a particular film, from actor through technician to director. The 1947 Boomerang represented an important turn for Hollywood from its rather "monotonous dreamland, into the illimitable possibilities of the world the eye actually sees."[24] Agee's reverence for reality was revealed in his first publication, the collection of poetry Permit Me Voyage, and in all of his subsequent works, through the posthumously published A Death in the Family. He maintains that if freed from the thrice-removed studio sets, the actors would be provoked into performing more plausibly because of the bracing encounter with reality. Richard Schickel, on the same premise, claims that this type of influence took place in David Lean's Brief Encounter. What could have been just an ordinary minor film achieves tension by Lean's positioning the romantic story of a touching, doomed love affair against a series of dreary, sordid backgrounds.[25] The atmosphere impacts the film with a gritty, plausible quality; the players appear to have absorbed it.

24
   "The New Pictures," Time, XLIX (March 10, 1947), 97-98.

25
   Movies, the History of an Art and an Institution (New York, 1964), p. 147.

Certain directors have insisted on using actual locations.
Eisenstein so fiercely believed in location-shooting that as a young
theatre director he tried to stage a play about a strike in a factory.
It failed, but Eisenstein was sufficiently inspired to demand the
use of actual locations throughout his film career.[26] Satyajit Ray
also attests to the creative impact actual locations have had on his
films. Working in a strange but real environment opens a new and
fascinating world. Its unaccustomed flavor and texture stimulate
him to observe and probe, to catch the revealing details, the
expressive gestures, the individual turns of speech of the particular
locale.[27]

Agee's most thorough explanation of opposition to studio sets
and advocacy of actual locations occurs in the review of A Tree Grows
in Brooklyn.

> Yet A Tree Grows in Brooklyn is as much a
> disappointment -- even an annoyance -- as a
> pleasure. My heart goes out to the people
> who reproduced the Brooklyn street . . .
> but try as they will, they only prove, more
> convincingly because more masterfully than I
> have seen it proved before, that the best you
> can do in that way is as dead as an inch-by-
> inch description of a perfectly naturalistic
> painting, compared with the still scarcely
> imagined difficulties and the enormous
> advantages of submerging your actors in the
> real thing, full of its irreducible present
> tense and its unpredictable proliferations of
> energy and beauty (142).

26
    Ivor Montagu, Film World (Middlesex, 1964), p. 287.

27
    Pauline Kael, I Lost It At The Movies (Boston, 1966), p. 224.

There is little wonder that many directors and producers have
preferred working in the controlled conditions of a studio. Paul
Rotha reports that it is "fantastically difficult" to shoot a film
on location. Da Sica's Bicycle Thief illustrates the prohibitive
obstacles for a director since Da Sica had to have seeming control
over the very crowds and traffic of Rome. Having decided to set one
of the scenes in a torrential downpour, he had to be certain that in
the remaining sequences the streets and pavements were wet, so that
visual continuity would be preserved.[28] Luis Buñuel was harried
throughout the shooting of Los Olvidados in the slums of Mexico City.
In portraying a gang of juvenile delinquents in their actual
neighborhoods, he encountered interference from the local people and
from the Mexican motion picture industry, whose pictures tend to be
very slow, beautiful tourist attractions or whip-slashing melodramas.
As a result, Buñuel was forced to work quickly and roughly.[29] David
Lean, insisting on location-shooting for Lawrence of Arabia, endured
hardships almost equal to those experienced by Robert Flaherty in
filming Nanook of the North during an Arctic winter. Producers have
realized that in such circumstances costs can soar. In studio
productions, shooting can be tightly controlled and disciplined; so
many shots-per-hour, so much cut screen-time-per-day. In short, every

---

[28]
Rotha on Film (Fair Lawn, 1958), p. 145.

[29]
Penelope Huston, The Contemporary Cinema (Baltimore, 1965),
pp. 157-158.

aspect of a studio film is taped, scheduled, and card-indexed.[30]

Not all of the opposition has been commercial. The French
director Maurice Tourneur believes that the idea of sending a company
to Central America to film a Central American story is valueless from
the standpoint of art. It is sufficient for the artist to produce a
story so that the audience receives an artist's impression of tropical
America. Edward Wagenknecht expresses his sympathy, based on general
aesthetic principles, with this point of view.[31] Meyer Levin sees no
aesthetic reasons compensatory enough for encumbering the commercial
and environmental burdens of location-shooting. He states that it was
an experimental notion, mainly Agee's, to combine a costume film with
a documentary setting for the Lincoln television series. And, though
some of the quality of the Lincoln country seeps through in the shows,
"the expense of location shooting, with professional crew and actors,
often cramped the operation."[32] Agee, I am certain, would classify
Levin a "New York rustic," a disparaging term he employed, while
referring to his Lincoln scripts, in a letter to Father Flye.

> These scripts never quite finish. I'm now working
> on revisions of commentary. Meanwhile they have
> gone to Kentucky and Illinois to shoot the film.
> If, or when, I finish this work, I am supposed to
> be there as a consultant. I'd better be, or this

[30]
Rotha, p. 23.

[31]
Wagenknecht, pp. 210-211.

[32]
"Abraham Lincoln Through The Picture Tube," Reporter, VIII (April
14, 1953), 31-33.

whole thing will be the work of New York
rustics.[33]

Some film-makers err in thinking that the only ingredient
necessary to convey realism is an actual location. An entire street
full of litter and garbage cans, even if actual, somehow appears less
real on the screen than a street with one garbage can. Too much
detail can smother realism.[34] Michael Roemer, the director of Nothing
But A Man, experienced this phenomenon directly. A few scenes in his
film take place in the squalid, poverty-stricken attached houses of
the Negro district in Birmingham, Alabama. Before shooting, the
crew had to spend three days cleaning the houses so that they would
appear plausibly dirty and run-down, not overwhelmingly filthy as
they were in actuality. These finished scenes in the film appear
pitiably and depressingly "real."[35]

Agee dismisses the sometimes beautiful streets and interiors in
The Lodger because they draw "too much attention to their own

---

[33]
Letters of James Agee to Father Flye (New York, 1962), p. 185.

[34]
Hollis Alpert, The Dreams and The Dreamers (New York, 1962), p.250,
has a knowledgeable treatment of the elusiveness of realism in the
film.

[35]
In an interview with Peter Vollstadt, cameraman for Nothing But A
Man, on April 12, 1967, in Northport, New York, I admired the film's
realistic depiction of a Southern City's Negro district as one of
the finest on record. I discovered, during the interview, that the
Birmingham, Alabama, scenes were shot in the Negro section of Atlantic
City, New Jersey, because of budgetary limitations. This, of course,
does not detract from the film's success in so ably communicating the
illusion of reality.

sumptuous but very passive vitality." (76). His criticism maintains
a balance, never allowing the regard for actual locations to
overshadow the other more significant, thematic elements of a film.
The use of actual locations can possibly exert a creative influence
on actors and film-makers. This is the point missed by Jack Behar,
who, writing on Agee's call for location-shooting, charges that he
does not specify the relationship of background actuality to the
film as a whole. According to Behar, Agee would be satisfied with
the "tertiary realism" imparted to a film by the use of actual
locations.[36] What Agee does call for is the submerging of actors
and technicians into the real thing, with its liberating present
tense and its layers of unpredictable energy and tension. Agee
would accept Ivor Montagu's distinction that it is not the accumulation
of actual details (tertiary realism) and its treatment, but the story
which determines the degree of realism in a film. The Western, with
all of its actual exteriors of grass and cowhide, is still in the
genre of myth.[37]

Whether appraising the virtues of actual locations or the role
of the active camera, Agee maintains certain priorities. Film
techniques can enhance, not create, a great film. He makes this

[36]
Jack Behar, "James Agee: The World of His Work" (Ann Arbor, 1963),
p. 92. An unpublished dissertation from Ohio State University.

[37]
Montagu, p. 289.

position clear reviewing Holiday in Mexico, which "stimulates the
eye and ear, but gives the pulse and brain a good 127-minute rest."[38]
Intellect and emotions have to be engaged by a film, and the mechanical
elements should be directed to this end. Hitchcock's film The
Paradine Case fails, because it contains clever little shots-in-the-arm
that are unrelated to the story. Many tricks of lighting and mood
are somewhat effective but irrelevant.[39]

These views place Agee in the mainstream of film criticism. Ezra
Goodman reports with approval that although William Cameron Menzies,
Hollywood's foremost production designer during the 1930's and 1940's,
was paid to be preoccupied with technique, he was aware of the sterile
pitfalls into which technical wizardry per se can lead. He furthered
the cause of film mechanics, but not at the cost of sacrificing the
other more essential elements.[40]   It is faintly ironic that one of
the great technicians of Hollywood, which is world-renowned principally
for its technical mastery, should admit the priority of non-technical
elements. The fate of D. W. Griffith illustrates that even technical
genius can carry one only so far, and then the artist, in this most
public of arts, has to communicate to audiences ideas and emotions
which have genuine relevance.[41]   Sergei Eisenstein, acknowledged to be

[38] "Holiday in Mexico," Time, XLVIII (September 2, 1946), 92.

[39] "Leading Man," Time, LI (January 12, 1948), 52-56.

[40] The Fifty Year Decline and Fall of Hollywood (New York, 1962), p.301.

[41] Schickel, p. 53.

the master of film grammar because of his surpassing technical
command of the medium, insists that the principle of montage, as well
as the other technical principles, is to be used for the "emotional
dynamization of the subject," and not just for itself, lest it decay
into "stylistic mannerisms."[42]

Of the specific techniques of the film, none has aroused more
controversy than sound. From its introduction on a broad commercial
basis in the 1927 The Jazz Singer, the sound film has been rejected by
a number of theorists, who have insisted that sound detracts from the
art of the film. Rudolph Arnheim, in one of the bibles of film
aesthetics, declares that sound has a paralyzing effect. A continuous
flow of images with only sporadic dialogue causes a jarringly
intermittent parallelism. Any slowing down of the images for the sake
of the sound results in artistic loss.[43] In point of fact, most silent
films contain the constant, irritating interruptions of subtitles
(both dialogue and continuity) during which all movement is not just
partially paralyzed, but totally absent. Another noted theorist,
Ernest Lindgren, charges sound with overwhelming the visual aspect of
films. Directors often are tempted to let the words do the work,

[42]
Film Form and the Film Sense, ed. Jay Leda (Cleveland, 1957), p. 58.

[43]
Film as Art (Berkeley, 1966), pp. 229-230. It is interesting to
note, in connection with these "theorists," that D. W. Griffith prepared
elaborate musical scores, to be played, if possible, by symphony
orchestras, for his own silent films.

rather than the camera.[44]   And Edward Wagenknecht believes that the
medium, even with accomplishments like La Strada, Roshomon, and
The Seventh Seal, has artistically declined since the advent of
sound. To Luigi Pirandello, the language of the film is images, and
images do not speak.[45]   Kevin Brownlow, a young, practicing director
(the 1966 It Happened Here) and editor (Richardson's 1968 The Charge
of the Light Brigade), believes that the golden era of the silent
movies from 1916 to 1925 is the richest in the cinema's history,
before the novelty of sound revived the industry but killed an art.[46]

Agee leaves no doubt as to the extent of his admiration for the
silent screen. "Comedy's Greatest Era," recognized as the definitive
eulogy of silent screen comedians, in no way contradicts his basic
acceptance of sound as a technological advance. Sound does not
necessarily have to limit the visual quality of a film; it can, by
providing creative possibilities, enrich the medium. The 1945
Bewitched is remarkable only in that the director, Arch Oboler,

---

[44]
   The Art of the Film (New York, 1963), pp. 93-94.

[45]
   Wagenknecht, p. 7. It is surprising that this bit of semantic
sophistry comes from Pirandello, a student of philosophy and semantics:
images do not speak according to his definition. Pictures or images
did not speak prior to the invention of the motion picture camera,
so at one time it was possible to state that images do not speak. A
definition does not constitute an immutable law.

[46]
   Arthur Mayer, "The Parade's Gone By . . . ," The New York Times
(December 8, 1968), pp. 1; 58-60.

achieved the film's first effective use of internal monologue.[47] A
melodrama about double personality, the film counterpoints inner
voices with dialogue, and thus approximates a stream of consciousness
(171). In Warner Brothers' Possessed (1947), exaggerated rain,
distorted musical flashbacks and other imaginative uses of sound are
well suited to the story of a dazed derelict, suffering a form of
schizophrenia (373). Agee also praises Olivier's inventive uses of
sound in Hamlet: the frightfully amplified heartbeats which
introduce the Ghost and, more importantly, the asides and soliloquies
recorded on the sound track but played as mental monologues (391).

Other theorists and film-makers have responded to the advantages
of sound. As the stage rarely can, the film easily produces the exact
timbre of a sound. Steiner's playing Bach on a church organ in
Fellini's La Dolce Vita sounds precisely like a church organ in a
large cathedral, since the sound was recorded there. René Clair has
been credited with teaching the sound track how to behave, by demanding
that it go far beyond literalness. Once freed from literalness, sound
could serve many functions, and so eventually earned greater
acceptance by critics. Edward Fisher asserts that sound can add an
aesthetic dimension. The giant tree creaking in the cemetery sequence
in Great Expectations, for example, contributes to the mood, while

---

[47]
  "Bewitched," Time, XLVI (September 3, 1945), 91-92.

setting up audiences for the jolt of a little boy being grabbed by the gigantic man.[48]   More recently, Joseph Losey's Accident closes with a shot of the protagonist's English country house, while the sound track replays the sounds of the car crash which occurred in front of the house in the beginning of the film. The lives of the people in the house have been altered irrevocably by the crash.

Agee attempted creative uses in his own film scripts. Prior to the climactic fight in The Blue Hotel, the combatants and onlookers plunge into the violent weather outside the hotel. There are detailed instructions calling for the use of electronic sound, a quite avant-garde gesture when the script was written in 1948:

> The camera is medium close to the door,
> waist-high, shooting past the door toward the
> station, as they stumble out. FULL SOUND of
> a very strong wind, but more compelling than
> any other noise, a pure electric or electronic
> SOUND, without timbre, either so high it is
> just at the limit of audibility or so high that
> it is just beyond that limit and works purely
> on the nervous system.[49]

Because Agee realizes the creative potential of sound, he rails at one of its major abuses, a deluge of words. The text of Huston's "San Pietro" richly and flexibly points itself against the individual images so that for once, "wordiness in a film more than earns its way" (163). More typically, Hollywood directors allowed words to intrude upon and detract from the visual images, as the post-war film The Search illustrates: while starving children grab for bread,

---

[48]
    Fischer, p. 61.

[49]
    Five Film Scripts, p. 445.

lady commentator informs audiences that "they are hungry, and that
ne bread is bread" (302). Siegfried Kracauer similarly charges
ollywood with too often degrading individual, effective shots with
ome robust commentator's bombastic eloquence. In his study of Nazi
ropaganda, he states that the Nazis, in contrast to Hollywood, relied
n long pictorial sequences without any verbal comment.[50]

An unofficial, unproclaimed, yet palpably real, Hollywood ban
n silence exasperated Agee. After the establishment of sound,
roducers feared that the paying public would feel cheated if this
atest technological miracle was not in evidence every second during
film. With similar nose-length vision, producers in the 1900's at
irst resisted the use of close-ups, since they were fearful that the
ublic, having paid to see a whole actor, might object to seeing just
part of him.[51] Agee refers to Hollywood's fear of silence, much
n evidence in the 1940's, by calling attention to the difficulty of
ttaining lyrical eloquence in a film when silence is almost as taboo
n the screen as in radio.[52] Another reason for the general avoidance
f silence is Hollywood's reluctance to make the audience work.
Marshall McLuhan claims that with silent films we automatically provide
sound for ourselves by way of "closure" or completion. When it is
filled in for us, there is much less participation.[53] In the same

[50]
From Caligari to Hitler (Princeton, 1947), p. 206.

[51]
Schickel, pp. 140-141.

[52] "The New Pictures," Time, LI (March 17, 1948), 102-106.

[53] Understanding Media: The Extensions of Man (New York, 1964), p.287.

vein, Agee infers that most Hollywood films are produced with the
theory that the audience is passive and wants to remain passive:
"Every effort is made to do all the work -- the seeing, the explaining,
the understanding, even the feeling" (329). To begin to realize a
fraction of their potential, sound films have a simple lesson to
learn: "they have to know when to shut up" (155). Even with the
artistic gains made in the last twenty years, Hollywood has not
learned this lesson. Silence is still taboo. Conversely, many
foreign directors respect silence. Godard relies on the disquieting
combination of electronic effects and silence in Alphaville, his
vision of a futuristic, state-controlled society.

Agee is particular in noting films which creatively use silence.
Carl Dreyer's Day of Wrath works as closely as possible with the
absolutes of darkness, stasis, and silence. This achievement prompts
Agee to suspect that Gluck and Beethoven in their finest music were
acutely aware of silence (304). Alfred Hitchcock is acclaimed for
his "expressive little air-pockets of dead silence" (214). Silence
should be used, not because it tends to recapture the golden age of
the silent screen, but because of its inherent attributes. Contrary
to popular belief, silence exerts a positive influence in accentuating
the other elements of a film, notably the non-verbal means an actor has
of expressing character. Gestures, timing, facial expression, and
grouping all become intensified during a few silent frames.[54] Balázs
makes essentially the same point in distinguishing between the use

54
Wagenknecht, p. 8.

of silence on the stage and on the screen. The contrast of silence
upon a character's unexpected entrance into a noisy crowd on stage
can be dramatic, and yet if the silence is too prolonged, the pace
slackens. Silence can last much longer and be more vivid and varied
on the screen, since close-ups can focus on a silent glance, gesture,
or facial movement. Balázs with justification contends that in a
film "silence does not halt action even for an instant and such
silent action gives even silence a living face."[55]

Consistent with a call for the use of silence, Agee prefers a
background composed of natural sounds. Call Northside 777 superbly
utilizes sound; except in the Chicago dives where music is properly
heard, the soundtrack records only the evocative natural music of a
big city.[56] The counterpointing of composed music with natural sounds,
an implicit blend of realism and poetry, is also recognized. Desert
Victory contains two musical movements, the industrial build-up and
the build-up of the barrage, which are judiciously balanced with the
natural sounds, so that the screen's images are charged rather than
dissipated (34). The fusion of literal sound with evocative music
can create a direct emotional force, in contrast to the common
background music that usually sugar-coats images.

---

[55] Theory of the Film, trans. Edith Bone (New York, 1953), p. 207.
Agee, of course, was not writing a book of critical theory, like
Balázs, but reviewing particular films for periodicals: for Time he
had deadline pressure; for The Nation, he had none. In neither publication did he go into this kind of theoretical explication, nor was
he expected to. At times, as with the use of studio sets or musical
backgrounds, he did explore the theory involved. At other times,
though, he used terms carelessly or made puzzling statements without
an explanation.

[56] "The New Pictures," Time, LI (February 16, 1948), 99-101.

Occasionally, there have been creative or integral backgrounds.
For the night scene preceding the Battle of Agincourt in Olivier's
Henry V, the camera scans the opposed camps. There are no natural
sounds like neighing steeds or clanking armor. Instead, William
Walton's original score provides "subdued, musical metaphors" (364).
By heightening the anticipation of battle, the score performs a
dramatic function. Antonioni believes that the music in L'Avventura
was used in a meaningful way, and not just as a kind of external
commentary on the action, like the Hollywood practice of injecting
violin pieces for sad scenes and violent symphonic crescendoes for
battle scenes. In L'Avventura, the music was intended to complement
the images by intensifying their meaning. Antonioni wanted the music
in itself to express what the images expressed, so that it would be
an integral part of the image.[57]   In his own film scripts, Agee
reveals an impatience, similar to Antonioni's, with the customary uses
of film music. He includes elaborate instructions in Noa-Noa for the
funeral of Pomare, the Tahitian king. Certain shots are to be cut to
Chopin's "Funeral March," which is to be played in the style of a
French provincial military band of the period, "rather shrill and
squeaky, and not very well."[58]   The further contrasting of native
shrieks, in the form of a dirge, with Chopin's music is intended to
create a weird, supernatural effect.

---

[57]
"Two Statements," in Film Makers on Film Making, ed. Harry M.
Geduld, pp. 195-223.

[58]
Five Film Scripts, p. 61.

Agee's credo for the use of music in films is included in the

review of John Huston's "San Pietro."

> Music can be well used in movies. It was
> wonderfully used in Dovzhenko's Frontier, for
> instance; for another I like the naïve,
> excitable, perfectly appropriate score of the
> soundtracked version of The Birth of a Nation;
> and indeed I think the greatest possibilities
> have hardly yet been touched. But music is
> just as damaging to nearly all fiction films
> as to nearly all fact films, as it is generally
> used in both today. Its ability to bind
> together a succession of images, or to make
> transitions between blocks of them -- not to
> mention 'transitional' and 'special-effect' and
> 'montage' passages -- inevitably makes for
> laziness or for slackened imagination in making
> the images and setting them in order, and in
> watching them. Still worse, it weakens the
> emotional imagination both of maker and onlooker,
> and makes it virtually impossible to communicate
> or receive ideas. It sells too cheaply and far
> too sensually all the things it is the business
> of the screen itself to present (164).

Instead of underscoring and intensifying the emotional content of

images, music too often has been used to compensate for a lack of

emotion in the images. It also can, by an emotional sales pressure,

diminish any deeply felt emotion. In The Clock, a soldier and a girl

in the beginning of the film walk, as if hypnotized, into their first

embrace. The timing of their walk and the increasingly large

close-ups are effectively bold. Even a suggestion of death in the

soldier's face is achieved. Yet during all of this, "with the

dirtiest and most merciless kind of efficiency, a full orchestra and

hyped-up soprani are working at you, below the belt" (165). Director

Minelli, by not trusting in the scene itself to generate a sufficient

response, ironically diminished, by such a blatant use of music,

the emotion inherent in the scene.

Many musical scores detract from and intrude on the realism in films. The bone-chilling, free-for-all fight in an alcoholic ward in The Lost Weekend, which could be all but stupefying, is enfeebled by a relentlessly loud use of background music (182). Even though there is relatively little music in The Treasure of The Sierra Madre, and some of it is better than average, there should be absolutely none for such a stark, unembellished study of the rawer experiences of reality. Agee adds that he could only hope and assume that John Huston fought its use (293). Three years after writing this, Agee collaborated with Huston on The African Queen. The London Philharmonic, prominently billed in the opening title credits of that film, is permitted, with full orchestra but no "hyped-up soprani," to intrude on a few scenes which would be more gripping if played silently or without music. One wonders if Agee fought this use of music, or if he himself was immune to the corruption he had previously described.

A significant number of other critics balk at the use of standard background music. Ernest Lindgren, with a too sweeping condemnation, claims that it is "a gross offense against reason and good taste." Further, intrusive background music has caused such widespread irritation that it is difficult to understand why the habit has persisted.[59] Edward Fischer more reasonably charges that some directors seem to fear a little honest silence, because they feel a

[59]
    Lindgren, p. 138.

loaded soundtrack can hide a multitude of artistic sins.[60] Paul

Rotha advocates an austere theory that permits only music which

logically has its source in the story: a street-band, a song, a

radio, a cafe musician. All other background music should be banned.[61]

Agee would be disposed to agree with Rotha's position, in the face

of such overwhelming misuse of music, yet he would oppose the

finality of the prohibition, which does not allow for exceptions.

In the 1960's, Agee would have many occasions to endorse the

use of music in films. A harpsicord contributes to the high spirits

in Tony Richardson's Tom Jones and assists in establishing a rowdy

Eighteenth Century background. Bo Widerberg in Elvira Madigan

parallels the exquisite theme of a Mozart piano concerto with the

fragile, poignant love of Elvira and her lover, suggesting that

anything so intensely beautiful must be short-lived. In Arthur Penn's

Bonnie and Clyde, Clyde, in a playful demonstration for Bonnie's

sake, robs a hardware store. They then roar down a dirt road in a

stolen car, having the time of their lives, while the sound track

blasts carefree, exhilarating banjo music. Much later in the film,

after their gang has been ambushed, Bonnie and Clyde, badly wounded

and half-dead, barely manage to escape in a stolen car, and are

driven down a dirt road by their accomplice. The same banjo music

is played in a slower, somber tempo to ironically comment on the "fun"

60
 Fischer, p. 63.

61
 Rotha, p. 23.

in leading such lives.

Editing has been considered by some theorists to be the
foundation of the art of the film. Though not esteemed so highly by
Agee, he does consider it one of the most crucial technical aspects.
He thinks of it in terms of the rhythm, pacing, and variations in
stress which exist in poetry. The British documentary <u>Desert Victory</u>
approaches the poetic, principally by its "internal rhyming," which
is not explained by Agee. I suspect that he means the images are
joined pictorially and progress smoothly and regularly; there are no
posterish or studied effects. This documentary also reveals the
possibilities intrinsic to editing: the power of film images in
themselves and in juxtaposition, in series, and in a rhythmic and
spatial whole. In contrast, the average nonfiction film moves "in
great blotches of ill-punctuated gabble, filled with uh's, ah's, and
as-I-was sayings" (33-34). Agee demands of editing, as of poetry,
a logical cadence with an inner consistency.

Editing consists of two separate operations. The order, length,
and type of individual shots are decided in the first stage, before the
work of the second stage begins in the actual cutting room. Agee
proceeds on this knowledge in a detailed analysis of the editing
skills of John Huston, who excels in the first place but fails in the
second. Huston's shots are not buttered together, Hollywood style,
but are "cantilevered, sprung together in electric arcs." His scenes
are often composed of off-beat alternations of rhythm and patterns of
exchange between long, medium, and close shots, and between the fixed,

tracking and dollying camera (329). Though not sufficiently
clarifying the two stages of editing for his readers and thereby
causing some confusion, Agee finds fault with huston's handling of
the actual cutting. By the time his films reach the stage of
refinement in the cutting room, he seems to lose interest. Often,
he allows others to do the final cut, which Agee rightly terms a
startling irresponsibility. The final stage, however tedious, is
essential because, in effect, it is the proofreading which determines
whether the alternations of camera positions and length of shots
create the rhythm and pace envisioned in the first stage. Agee
would accept totally Cocteau's theory regarding the second stage of
cutting. "That is the key to my work. My handwriting. No one else
can do it for me."[62] With this viewpoint, Cocteau and Agee are in
the minority. The bulk of directors are more like Huston than
Cocteau.

Agee also perceives in editing the order and emotional impact of
good poetry. The British mystery I Met a Murderer is recognized as
the product of judicious ordering: the makers obviously cared how
each shot follows the next, and what in the way of emotion,
atmosphere, observation, and psychological weight and progression
each shot, as well as each series of shots, contains (150). The
Adventures of Tartu has editing "as shrewdly varied as that of a
roller coaster"; in this case, an emotional response is effected by

62
Cocteau, p. 178.

the carefully controlled changes from painfully slow suspense to breathtaking speed.[63] In a similar vein, Slavko Vorkapich compares the alternating and ordering of shots to the visual displacement brought about by a sudden close-up. By selecting shots or designs and intercutting them in various ways, a purely filmic force can create an intense visual impact.[64] Ernest Lindgren views editing as involving a complex set of relationships between the individual shots, as well as relationships of idea, duration, physical movement, and form. By skillful manipulation, the director can control the emotional tone of a scene.[65]

Precisely because of these attributes, editing has been declared the essence of cinematic art. The Russian directors of the 1920's in particular were vocal in support of this claim. In contrast, Agee reports that the American documentary Tunisian Victory contains superb editing in that the shots and clusters of shots are as fine as can be imagined, and yet they never gather momentum nor are they in themselves enough to overcome the nagging commentary (84). Even with extraordinary cutting, this work does not succeed as cinema. However expert, editing can not impart greatness to a work. V.I. Pudovkin, on the

---

[63] "The New Pictures," Time, XLII (September 20, 1943), 94-96.

[64] Slavko Vorkapich, "Toward True Cinema," in Introduction to the Art of the Movies, ed. Lewis Jacobs, 288-296.

[65] Lindgren, p. 80.

other hand, writes that "the foundation of film art is editing."[66]

It is the creative force of the cinema because it psychologically

guides viewers from one frame to the next. Eisenstein attaches the

same importance to editing: through the juxtaposition of two shots,

a third image or force is created different from, and more important

than, the content of the two individual shots.[67] To Eisenstein,

montage is the metaphor of film language. Both men agree that what

takes place in front of the cameras is mere recording, not art. A

director in the cutting room is the purest example of a film artist.

With the advent of sound, both theorists have insisted adamantly,

if somewhat foolhardily, that editing, even in the new era, remains

the essence of cinema.[68]

In addition to the Russian directors, many other film theorists

have assigned the same importance to editing. Ernest Lindgren argues

that soulless photographs (the individual shots) have to be given

cinematographic life through the chemistry of editing.[69] Agee would

---

[66]
Pudovkin, p. 23.

[67]
Eisenstein, pp. 247-249. In France and other European countries, montage is generally synonomous with cutting; Eisenstein prefers to think of montage in the specific terms of juxtaposing two shots to create a third force.

[68]
Pudovkin, p. 199.

[69]
Lindgren, p. 20.

retort that photographs, or individual shots, do not have to be soulless. The content of the shots, rather than their ordering, pacing, or rhythm, is what most matters. Raymond Spottiswoode likewise claims that the very grammar of the film is editing, or the mode of transition from one shot to the next, because it controls the extremely important spatial transitions.[70] George Bluestone, somewhat anachronistically for a theorist of the late 1950's, proposes that the principle of montage, enunciated first by the Russian directors, "is as central today as it was in its infancy."[71] Agee, however, insists that editing is no more than one of the most vital technical functions of the film.

In a classic statement on film aesthetics, Erwin Panofsky declares that the process of editing endows the film medium with unique and specific possibilities, which he defines as "the dynamization of space, and the spatialization of time."[72] Pudovkin writes that filmic space and filmic time are distinct from real space and real time. The material of the film director consists not of events occurring in real space and time, but of those pieces of

---

[70]
A Grammar of the Film (Berkeley, 1965), p. 202.

[71]
Novels into Film (Berkeley, 1966), p. 18.

[72]
Erwin Panofsky, "Style and Medium in the Motion Pictures," in Film: An Anthology, ed. Daniel Talbot (Berkeley, 1966), p. 19.

celluloid on which the events have been recorded.[73] Maya Deren

believes the time-space factor is the heart of the medium, and

defines cinema as "A timespace art with a unique capacity for

creating temporal-spatial relationships and projecting them with an

incontrovertible impact of reality."[74] All of these theorists have

the same message: the film director can create a new illusion of

reality by being able to make the laws of time and space, ordinarily

invariable, tractable and flexible.

Agee tends to treat the concepts of space and time in more of an

impressionistic manner than is his custom. He deals more with the

liberation of time than with space, evidently for personal preference,

since in theory they are of equal significance. The fictional war

film Objective Burma closes with a long sequence of a night attack,

which communicates the agony of long waiting -- what seems like

hours -- in the matter of a minute or two of screen time. As the

darkness swarms in with the enemy, the screen is so dark audiences are

almost as confused as the soldiers, and the sound track is silent

long enough to suggest the heaviness of anticipation and fear weighing

on the waiting combatants.[75] Agee suggests more than he explains

about the time factor in The Treasure of the Sierra Madre. He

relegates to parentheses a perceptive comment, which should have been

[73]
  Pudovkin, p. 84.

[74]
  Maya Deren, "Cinema as an Art Form," in Introduction to the Art of
the Movies, ed. Lewis Jacobs, pp. 262-263.

[75]
  "Objective Burma," Time, XIV (February 26, 1945), 92-94.

clarified: "...or subtler and more skillful collusions and
variations in tempo (two hours have certainly never been better used
in a movie)." He has in mind, I believe, the obsessive greed of the
Bogart character, which serves as catalyst for certain variations in
tempo: the fever pitch of work associated with the initial discovery
of gold, the numbing slowness, particularly the all-night vigil, when
suspicion dominates. Agee similarly mentions, without explanation,
Jean Vigo's slow-motion pillow fight in "Zero de Conduite." By
distending time and flooding the screen with pillow feathers slowly,
unnaturally descending, from the pillows ripped during the fight, Vigo
is able to cast a dream-like, ritualistic quality over this scene.

Sergei Eisenstein, acclaimed by all theorists for his control
over space and time effects in the film, protracts time by means
different from Vigo. He capitalizes on the ability of the film to
literally play with the fourth dimension, time, without destroying a
sense of reality. No director in the history of film has been more
daring in varying screen time (the time it takes for an incident to
occur on the screen) from chronological time. The charge of the
Cossacks down the Odessa steps in Potemkin is an inspired piece of
time manipulation. What would take a matter of seconds in real time
is lingered over for minutes in order to isolate and focus upon
individual bits of action occurring during the mass chaos. [76] Agee

---

[76]
    Though this scene is admittedly a brilliant piece of editing, and
rightly used to illustrate filmic time manipulation, one must keep in
perspective the fact that the art of the film did not begin and end on
the Odessa steps.

again proves to be the perceptive, though impressionistic, critic in his only reference to this scene: these few minutes are as brilliantly organized as a movement in a Beethoven symphony. He aptly compares the genius of both artists for structuring, interweaving, and repeating themes, without monotony, in an inevitable progression toward a climax.

The stop shot is another device by which film-makers control time. Alexander Dovzhenko, a master of this technique, sometimes arrests motion for a picture which, like a still, presents some fragment of motionless reality. Kracauer, in a statement which seems to be more of an exaggeration than an accurate appraisal, views the stop-shot as a process for bringing life to a standstill so as to penetrate to the core of reality.[77]   All in an instant seems disclosed. Agee, on the other hand, more accurately considers the stop-shot a device basic to poetic resource. He points out that D. W. Griffith employed it with notable success in The Birth of a Nation. Rene Clair's masterful use in The Crazy Ray is referred to, again without explanation, but the reference is clear to anyone who has seen Clair's film. In this short comedy, a mad scientist invents a ray which can suspend all motion. A climactic struggle for control of the ray-producing machine results in the lever being shoved on and off. By imaginative injections of stop-shots, Ray throws all of Paris into an alternating dither of motion and paralysis. Manipulating time and motion by stop-shots can effect poignancy as readily as comedy. Near the end

[77]
From Caligari to Hitler, p. 302.

of newsreels of Iwo Jima, the camera slowly moves down a still of

dead soldiers, "for whom time no longer moved" (151). Agee's

enthusiasm for Georges Rouquier's use of stop shots in _Farrebique_

is expressed unequivocally:

> He uses stop-motion as I have always wanted to
> use it: very plainly, to show the motions of
> darkness and light and shadow; and with complete
> freedom and daring, in his orgiastic sequence on
> spring, to show the jubilant rending and pouring
> upward and blossoming of the world (298).

This endorsement in the 1940's for the use of stop-shots, rarely

used at that time, was somewhat visionary in the light of its

extensive use in contemporary cinema. François Truffaut's stop-shot,

in the last frame of _The 400 Blows_, of the child running next to the

ocean, imprisons a small, frightened boy in environmental conditions

beyond his control. Tony Richardson's stop-shot of protagonist Smith,

demoted to menial bench work after intentionally and defiantly losing

the Governor's race, shatteringly concludes _The Loneliness of the_

Long Distance Runner, as well as Smith's future.[78] Resnais, Godard,

and Varda also freely employ stop-motion, as do the directors of the

American Underground Cinema movement. Robert Downey, considered one

of its most promising directors, relegates in _Chafed Elbows_ some forty

percent of running time to stop motion. This is an extreme, if not

absurd, example; with so many stop shots, they lose any startling or

outstanding effect. The change-of-pace changes nothing.

78
  If the trend continues, we shall witness an excellent device, the
stop-shot as conclusion of a film, being turned into cliché. A few
recent examples of the practice are: _A Thousand Clowns_, _The Legend_
of Lylah Clare, _Elvira Madigan_.

Sir Herbert Read warns, if a little melodramatically in order
to make a valid point, that the film's freedom with time and space
threatens its existence. The problem of the film as an art form can
be reduced to its invention of proper conventions. It has to reject
the unities proper to drama and discover the unities proper to "a
space-time continum." He defines the film as essentially alogical.
Events can occur simultaneously: they can be represented in more than
one unit of dimension, and time itself can be controlled. The only
unity in the film is continuity.[79] With the intervening years,
directors like Fellini and Resnais have made discontinuity a basic
part of the flow of film images. In the process, time and space have
become even more pliable.

Agee feels that Olivier's Hamlet is a superb illustration of the
creation of a "kind of continum of time and space" (390). There is
no clear placement of time and seemingly no exterior world outside
the cavernous castle except the deliberate use of pathetic fallacies
such as blind sky, faint landscapes, ruminant surf, a lyrical brook.
Years prior to his criticism, Agee was sensitive to this filmic form.
In Let Us Now Praise Famous Men, he informs the reader that he is
shifting ahead to write of a thing which happened the next morning.
He adds, in parentheses, "you mustn't be puzzled by this, I'm writing
in a continuum."[80] More accurately, he was attempting to write in a
continuum. Like countless other writers, Agee desired to break free

---

[79] "Towards a Film Aesthetic," Cinema Quarterly, Vol. I (Autumn 1932), 7-11.

[80] Let Us Now Praise Famous Men, p. 62.

of the sequential, linear boundary of print to approximate the simultaneous flow of images in the film medium.

Space and time have constantly interacted. Since time has great flexibility in the film, space attains proportionately more mobility.[81] The liberation of space admits a world of possibilities. Panofsky points out that not only bodies move in space, but space itself does,[82] approaching, receding, turning, dissolving, and recrystallizing. Agee's essay on silent comedy reveals a technical, appreciative awareness of the anarchic, law-transgressing practices responsible for so much of the fun associated with the silent films of Mack Sennett.

> Realizing the tremendous drum-like power of mere motion to exhilarate, he gave inanimate objects a mischievous life of their own, broke every law of nature the tricked camera would serve him for and made the screen dance like a witches' Sabbath. The thing one is surest of all to remember is how toward the end of nearly every Sennett comedy, a chase built up such a majestic trajectory of pure anarchic motion that bathing girls, cops, comics, dogs, cats, babies, automobiles, locomotives, innocent bystanders, sometimes what seemed like a whole city, an entire civilization, were hauled along head over heels in the wake of that energy like dry leaves following an express train (6).

The tractability of space can contribute equally well to more serious films. Agee singles out John Huston for his delicate, simple feeling for space relationships: the camera moves in closely on characters huddling to talk, and stays back at a relaxed middle distance for those casually talking. Unlike the theater, there is no

---

[81] Bluestone, p. 53.

[82] Panofsky, p. 19.

constancy of distance between viewer and action in the cinema, so
that film directors have another means of shaping plastic materials.
With the general breakdown of objective, sequential art over the past
four decades, contemporary directors have made more adventurous use
of this unrestricted time and space. No longer do only pioneers,
like Griffith, Vigo, or Clair, sculpt space and time effects.

The use of color, the final technical area under consideration,
has become increasingly more sophisticated and significant over the
past twenty years. William Johnson is correct in stating that until
the early 1950's most critics dismissed color movies as "garish,
pretty-pretty, or otherwise inartistic," while the public flocked to
them.[83] An exception is Agee, whose degree of acceptance increased
as the process of color evolved during the early 1940's. One of the
first reviews of a color film, dated November 2, 1942, playfully
dismisses color as Hollywood's latest toy. Technicolor makes the
landscapes of the U.S. Northwest look as handsome and healthy as
"skookum apples." What relation this lovely color has to the total
film is, of course, irrelevant. The review concludes with a postscript.
"Technical note: a forest fire looks fine in Technicolor. An actor,
after completing a lipsticky kiss, looks gruesome."[84] Some
eight months later there is a slightly discernible shift in viewpoint.
Color is very nice for costume pieces and musical comedies, but it

---

[83]
"Coming to Terms with Color," Film Quarterly, XX (Fall 1966),
2-22.

[84]
"The Forest Rangers," Time, XL (November 2, 1942), 97.

destroys any serious attempt at an imitation of reality. Agee
ventures so far as to grant, contrary to most of his contemporary
critical colleagues, that color probably has an aesthetic future in
films (48). Shortly after this review, an American war record film
successfully fused color and reality. Agee seems unprepared for its
impact: "The very rawness of the color helps to give a rawer reality
to some of the most real things ever fixed by a camera."[85] A year
later, however, his former doubts are again evidenced, as though the
war documentary proved to be an isolated example. In an October, 1945,
review, he accuses a film of turning a decent novel into one of the
most eye-drugging jobs of color on record,[86] while an early 1946 film
is pitied for being "saddled with technicolor."[87]

   Some three years after his first review of color, Agee accepted
it as an asset. The Raider, a British war fiction film, gains in
immediacy and reality by blending the beauty of color with the
imperfections of men and open nature (224). In perceiving this type
of counterpointed use of color, he anticipated the symbolic and
dramatic use of color by the directors of the 1960's. A few times,
however, Agee commended a particular film of the 1940's for in part
realizing its enormous potential. The sepia color of an historical

[85]
   "With the Marines at Tarawa," Time, XLIII (March 20, 1944), 94.
[86]
   "Frenchman's Creek," Time, XLIV (October 9, 1944), 94-96.
[87]
   "The Virginian," Time, XLVII (April 29, 1946), 94-96.

film gives the impression that everything is viewed as through a
blear of centuries (384). Vincente Minelli's use of color in Meet
Me in St. Louis was instrumental in the film's reflecting an age.
The "sober mahoganies and tender muslins and benign gas lights"
distill enough of the essence of the turn of the century to fill the
screen (356). Director Minelli further drew from color its
atmospheric qualities. The scene with a shot of a fine black horse
and buggy in a brisk and resonant autumn night diffuses "a cider
fragrance" (126).

Though a majority of earlier critics dismissed color on aesthetic
grounds, there were a select number who saw in the use of color
symbolic and dramatic possibilities. Balázs listed many dramatic
functions color can perform in the structure of a story, in addition
to its ability "of extending microphysiognomics." Subtle color changes
in the eyes of a major character can express inner emotions not easily
conveyable by other means.[88]   Although Balázs strains his thesis on
this point, he ranks with Agee, in the history of film criticism, as
one of the few theorists who accepted color. Another early advocate
was Eisenstein, who maintained that the silent film cries out for
sound in the same way that the sound film cries out for color.[89]   He

---

[88]
    Balázs, p. 243.

[89]
    Eisenstein, p. 121. As evidenced by the considerable number of
serious films in the late 1960's made in black and white, Eisenstein's
insight is still ahead of the times. Peter Ustinov, director of the
critically acclaimed Billy Budd, said he used black and white to impart
a greater sense of reality to the film. The implication is equivalent
to Agee's initial reaction that color detracts from the illusion of
reality.

also detailed at length the symbolic overtones which can be conveyed
by means of color. Particular colors can exert specific influence
on viewers, like the connection of yellow with sin. Once this
relationship is established, a director can key various scenes or
moments in this color. In the 1940's, Jean Cocteau also perceived
the wonders possible with the use of color. Filming <u>The Beauty and
the Beast</u>, he lamented that France was not able to afford color films.
"The arrival of Beauty at the wash-house, wearing her grand sky-blue
dress, surrounded by black chickens was an absolute miracle."[90]   As a
poet, Cocteau intuitively and simply accepted color. Learned theses
on the acceptability of color would appear irrelevant to him.

As Agee foresaw twenty years ago, color in the 1960's has become
established as a medium for the telling of visual stories. Many of
the foremost contemporary film-makers are now employing color not only
to set a tone or mood, like the earlier directors, but to reveal
character and to establish theme. Michelangelo Antonioni, who
declares that he will never make another film in black and white,
ingeniously uses colors in <u>Blow-Up</u> to spotlight his view of mod London
as a disoriented, topsy-turvy world. The film begins and ends with
the appearance of gaily decorated masqueraders, who no longer pretend
<u>not</u> to masquerade. These are among the few honest members of a
superficial, sleek society. Other touches, by the use of color,
reinforce the central theme. In the opening frames, two nuns, with
skin as black as their starkly white habits, walk down the street.

---

[90]
  Cocteau, p. 35.

This reversal of the usual white nuns in black habits suggests, by its incongruity, that the time is out of joint. In The Bride Wore Black (1968), Truffaut dresses his bride, whose husband was killed on the steps of a church after their wedding, only in black or white, or with a combination of black and white. No shades of color are used. Her stark appearance symbolizes the monomaniacal revenge which drives her to pursue and murder those men responsible for the death of her husband.

Alain Resnais superbly integrates color to help convey and heighten the theme of Night and Fog, his documentary about a Nazi concentration camp. Black and white accentuate the actual horrors of the wartime footage taken at the camp, while color bathes the postwar scenes of the camp, overgrown with weeds, quiet and peaceful in the sunlight. The harsh black and white sharpen the horror scenes in contrast to the affable colors of the other segments. These interjections of color scenes serve another function. They tend to ward off the numbing effect which can easily overcome audiences watching, for an extended period of time, without any break, one horror heaped on top of the other.

Years earlier, Agee outlined a strikingly similar alternation of color with black and white in Noa-Noa. Gauguin, near death in his Tahitian hut, holds before him a photograph of his family as they were many years ago in Paris. The photograph is shown in black and white so that the distance and time which separate Gauguin and his family seem even more pronounced and insurmountable. In this way, the contrast of black and white with color helps to communicate

Gauguin's realization of the profound, irreversible alteration he
brought upon his life, now drawing to a close.[91] By employing color
to reveal character and theme, Agee anticipated in his own film
scripts the coming of age of color, just as he proved to be one of
the few earlier critics to foresee its aesthetic potentialities.

Although understanding and appreciating the intricacies of the
mechanics of this relatively new electronic medium, Agee is too much
the poet and humanist to prefer the medium to the message. Whether
growing with the awkward development of color, or instructing the
uninitiated in the prowess of the camera, he never loses sight of the
fact that film techniques are not the raison d'etre of the film.
Agee's treatment of these techniques reveals a critic who is always
knowledgeable, often moderate, frequently progressive. Occasionally,
as in his own film scripts, he is experimental. At times, he, as
a critic, seems to be content to sketch an idea impressionistically
rather than to examine it analytically.

---

[91] Five Film Scripts, p. 143.

CHAPTER IV

THE ARTIST AS CRITIC

The thesis that Agee is the finest American film
critic rests not only on the basis of his esthetic, but
on his expression of that esthetic. Since his theories
concerning the film medium, a film style, and film
techniques have been examined, this chapter investigates
his individual method of expression. Even with a high
critical reputation, Agee has not been immune to censure.
In fact, it seems that condemnation has been the unjust lot
of film critics. R. G. Collingwood, a respected literary
critic, admits that while all critics are generally
despised, they ought rather to be pitied.[1] Film critics
have been peculiarly unfortunate in being the object of
attacks by former film critics such as William Zinsser,
Ezra Goodman, and Wolcott Gibbs, who claim to have
renounced film reviewing in order to preserve either their
integrity or their sanity. Mike Nichols, a young and most
successful representative of the artistic film community,
reaches the point of abusive irrationality in comparing
film critics to eunuchs in the sense that they contribute

---

[1]Collingwood, p. 91.

nothing of substance to the film medium.[2]

As a film critic, Agee has serious faults, but during
his eight years of film reviewing he lost neither his
integrity nor his sanity, and he did contribute to the
development of the art of film. He is the only American
film critic who, on the basis of his non-critical writings,
can be termed an artist. Let Us Now Praise Famous Men,
A Death in the Family, The Morning Watch, his poetry,
particularly the collection Permit Me Voyage, and the film
and television scripts comprise his small but significant
artistic accomplishments. Being an artist who writes or
directs the kind of works he criticizes does not
necessarily make one a better or more knowledgeable critic.
At least in Agee's case, it broadened his critical
sensibility and sympathy. Having experienced the
frustration of artistic creation,he was able to enter into
the texture, tone, and experience of the film under review.
Unlike Dwight Macdonald, Stanley Kauffmann, Pauline Kael
or Richard Schickel, Agee does not give the impression of
detachment, aloofness, or superiority. The dual role of
artist-critic is most discernible in his approach to, and
execution of, the actual writing of film criticism.

---

[2]Leslie Aldridge, "Who's Afraid of the Undergraduate?"
The New York Times Magazine, February 18, 1968, p. D15.

William Empson defines two types of critics, the
appreciator and the analyst.[3] Although it is demonstrable
that Agee in many ways is both analyst and appreciator,
his particular artistic temperment inclines decidedly
toward appreciation.

As appreciator, Agee's most notable attributes are a
love for and commitment to films. Five years before
becoming a critic, he complained that the Cukor film version
of Romeo and Juliet desecrates not Shakespeare, but the
movies. He was referring to the kind of embalmed
Shakespeare, stuffed with reverence and scholarship of
three hundred years, which reaches the movies.[4] In the
intellectual circles of 1936, such a statement was heresy.
This judgment did not proceed from a lack of admiration
for Shakespeare, as is clear in his praise, ten years later,
of Henry V, a film which honors the film medium as well as
Shakespeare.

> I am not a Tory, a monarchist, a Catholic,
> a medievalist, or an Englishman, or
> despite all the good it engenders, a
> lover of war; but the beauty and power of
> this traditional exercise was such that

[3]Empson, pp. 249-250.

[4]Letters of James Agee to Father Flye, pp. 85-86. Valid
in 1936, the statement in 1968 appears dated in view of the
exuberant, almost irreverent, Franco Zeffirelli
exaggerations of The Taming of the Shrew and Romeo and
Juliet. I think Agee would defend the spirit of the
undertakings, if not the actual productions.

> watching it, I wished I was, thought I
> was, and was proud of it. I was persuaded,
> and in part still am, that every time and
> place has since been in decline, save one,
> in which one Englishman used language
> better than anyone has before or since, or
> ever shall; and that nearly the best that
> our time can say for itself is that some
> of us are still capable of paying homage
> to the fact (212).

This passage reverberates with a love for more than just

the film. It reveals a sense of wonder and awe, as though

Agee had just encountered Shakespeare for the first time.

At its best, his prose is, in a sense, a celebration, an

act of discovering life and the world with joy.[5]

This appreciative approach directly contrasts with

many contemporary film critics. Dwight Macdonald, by his

own admission disgusted with current films, now writes only

political columns. Pauline Kael, who is more caustic than

accurate, dismisses such achievements as La Notte, Last

Year at Marienbad, and La Dolce Vita with the witticism,

"the come-dressed-as-the-sick-soul-of-Europe parties."[6]

Renata Adler manages, at only 29, to carry on Bosley

Crowther's stodgy tradition, by complaining in her New York

Times Sunday columns that films are worse than ever. In

addition, negativism can be found in Film Quarterly,

especially in the "Short Notices" section where "critics"

---

[5]R. Hayes, "Rhetoric of Splendor," Commonweal, LXVIII
(September 12, 1958), 591-592.

[6]I Lost It At The Movies. p. x.

vie to out-condemn the current crop of movies. I find Penelope Huston the only film critic at present who displays a generous and expansive spirit, even when negatively judging films.

Agee is passionate, intensely committed, often indignant. He occasionally is rude and troubling, and frequently over-steps the customary bounds of "good manners" in film-reviewing. Pauline Kael points out that the American film critic is in a curious position. The greater his interest in the film, the more enraged and negative he is likely to sound.[7] Agee's anger was ruled by his commitment, but, curiously, he was able to avoid that negative aura surrounding certain critics today. Many years prior to his career as a film critic, he expressed the opinion that irony, savage anger and even certain types of cynicism can, if used right, be as effective instruments and weapons as love, and are not incompatible with it.[8] Agee's criticism demonstrates this theory. The 1945 Shirley Temple film Kiss and Tell comes under savage attack because it superficially observes the letter of the production code while violating its spirit by exploiting sex at every opportunity:

---

[7]"Movies, the Desperate Art," in Film: An Anthology, ed. Dan Talbot (New York, 1959) p. 189.

[8]Letters of James Agee to Father Flye, p. 87.

> There is a plot held together only
> through the enormous stupidity,
> cowardice, and mean-heartedness of
> as ugly a bunch of suburban parents
> as have never yet got themselves done
> up brown, in any treatment worthy of
> them. It is all brilliantly
> characteristic of the worst anyone
> could think of American family life,
> and it is all clearly presented on
> the assumption that you will find it
> charming and sympathetic, and funny,
> because everyone in it is so exactly
> like you (178).

Such a personal, insulting passage is an instrument for
jolting the readers out of their complacency into a
realization of the abuse of the medium. Although many of
The Nation readers were relatively sophisticated, not the
smug bourgeois pictured in the movie, a large number would
still be included in Agee's censured group as "suburban
parents." Stanley Kauffmann correctly praises Agee for
abundantly possessing what is missing from all criticism
today, "fierce intensity." [9]

The primary reason for Agee's status as the finest
American film critic is his prose style, which, at its
best, reveals a poet's felicitous phrasing, and a
Southerner's rich rhetoric. The review of Farrebique is
representative of his finest critical prose. Georges
Rouquier, the director, is commended for inventive uses

---

[9]"Life in Reviews," New Republic, CXXXIX (December 1,
1958), 18-19.

of stop motion.

> He uses stop-motion as I have always
> wanted to use it: very plainly, to show
> the motions of darkness and light and
> shadow; and with complete freedom and
> daring, in his orgiastic sequence on
> spring, to show the jubilant rending
> and pouring upward and blossoming of
> the world (298).

Complete freedom and daring, ordinarily associated with

orgies, seem appropriate words to precede "orgiastic

sequence," and yet Agee's meaning in context is quite

different: orgiastic only in the sense of nature

celebrating its re-birth, which, once begun, proceeds at a

vertiginous pace. The oxymoron "jubilant rending" places

the pain or distress connected with rending in joyous

context. To climax the sentence, Agee follows "jubilant

rending" with "pouring upward," an uncomplicated yet

unexpected reversal: it is because the rain and sun pour

down upon the earth that spring responds with a pouring

upward of flowers and trees. The sentence sensibly ends

with the "blossoming of the world." After "orgiastic

sequence," "jubilant rending," and "pouring upward,"

Agee prudently chose to employ a simple, often used figure,

rather than risk cloying the effect of the sentence with

yet another reversal or unusual figure of speech.

Later in the same review, Agee notes the success

Rouquier had in being able to reproduce exactly the

various lights in the world.

> The film is full of lovely achievements:
> subdued autumnal light in which the
> whole world is as scratchily distinct as
> trillions of little briars; the veiled
> shining of spring; the supernal light
> beneath impounded thunder; the holy
> light of snow (299).

Adjectives carry the meaning for all except the first kind
of light mentioned. I suspect Agee was fearful that
"subdued autumnal light" by itself, unlike his later three
descriptions, would fail to communicate his meaning. So,
at the price of violating parallelism, he adds a simile.
Subdued is to be understood as hazy, not distinct; the
world is only as scratchily distinct as trillions of little
briars, which, because of the enormity of their number,
would begin to blur and merge upon examination. The phrase
"scratchily distinct" also suggests a grainy, not precise,
photographic quality.

The remaining three descriptions as effectively, yet
more economically, present Agee's distinctions. The
"veiled shining" of spring is sufficient to suggest the
mist-like effect of a vernal day, lush and heavy with
green. The "supernal light beneath impounded thunder" is
vague, yet rich with implications: supernal light comes
from above, yet Agee says beneath thunder. Actually, there
is no light beneath or in thunder. He means the
intermittent bursts of electricity which accompany the
"impounded" thunder.

Both the light and thunder are imprisoned, freed only for
brilliant bursts. The "holy light" of snow comes closest
to cliché, in the association of virgin snow. The phrase
does suggest the steady radiance of snow and its sanctuary-
like qualities of peace, stillness, and silence. Taken as
a whole, the sentence progresses logically through
gradations of light, from subdued to veiled to supernal to
radiant. The inner consistency of the sentence reinforces
the main point of the Farrebique review, that Rouquier
achieved an inspired film through discipline, order, and
poetic intelligence.

Some critics have been more astute than Agee in their
judgments, and others have been more knowledgeable about
the specifics of the medium, but no American film critic
has surpassed his prose style. Such quality in writing is
found in novels and poetry, but it is not expected or
found in film criticism.[10] Widely circulated is the story
that the editors of The Nation invited Agee, when seeing

---

[10]Renata Adler, "If You Enjoy It, It's Good Enough," The
New York Times, March 17, 1968, p. D1. Miss Adler harshly
charges that the language of movie reviewing is debased.
Ironically, she contributes to it, as did her predecessor,
Bosley Crowther. Although not on a level with Agee's,
most prose being written by film critics such as Kael,
Alpert, Knight, Schickel, and Huston is respectable, not
debased.

so many movies became too great a strain for him, to go on
writing whether he saw the movies or not, because they
wanted to print prose of such quality. W. M. Frohock, in
referring to this story, thinks it apocryphal, but adds
that it must have been started by someone who knew prose
of quality when he saw it.[11]

Agee's achievement in prose may be in part attributed
to an intuition for the right word. The portrait of a boss
in The Best Years of Our Lives could have been
unprecedented, trenchant satire for an American movie, but
instead it is the type of safe, clever caricature which,
like much of Gilbert and Sullivan, "makes every punch a
kind of self-caress" (230-231). Such an apt, pin-pointed
comparison conveys this particular brand of self-deception,
on the part of the producers, simply and crisply. Agee's
word choice at times proves delightful, like this
description of typical Mack Sennett slapstick: "a
profusion of hearty young women in disconcerting bathing
suits, frisking around with a gaggle of insanely
incompetent policemen" (5). Out of context, the words
"hearty," "frisking," and "gaggle" may seem a bit studied,
yet within the flow of "Comedy's Greatest Era" they serve
to re-create the feeling and flavor of those zany moments

---

[11]Frohock, p. 233.

on film. In concluding his three-part <u>Monsieur Verdoux</u> review for <u>The Nation</u>, Agee again displays a precise diction. If other conditions had prevailed for the unfortunate wife of Monsieur Verdoux, she might have lived contentedly in poverty, and "in the intactness of soul and the irresponsibility of that anarchic and immortal lily of the field, the tramp" (262). Agee's biblical allusion to Chaplin's most famous character creation is appropriate. The "intactness of soul" declares that the tramp can not be bribed or compromised by the world's materialism, which is irrelevant to him. "Irresponsibility" and "anarchic" express the tramp's happy lack of order, responsibility, or anxiety, because he has the immortality vouchsafed to the lily of the field.

Although not an unusually gifted writer in his early years,[12] Agee years before his period of film reviewing revealed the poet's penchant for the right word - sometimes on the most mundane subjects assigned by <u>Fortune</u>. In an unsigned, still largely unknown 1937 piece for <u>Fortune</u>, "Six Days at Sea," (among his finest work in any genre or medium), he satirically describes the frenetic American

---

[12]Father Flye in a personal interview stated that Agee showed no unusual promise as a writer while in high school. An examination of Agee's unpublished letters (and essay exams) during this period supported Father Flye's judgment.

tourists, off to Cuba on a luxury liner, determined, at all costs, to have a fun-filled vacation as the tour pamphlets promised. Towards the end of the article, Agee focuses on a young couple seated at a table in the dining area.

> A wife and husband sat in a dark corner talking intensely; two phrases kept re-emerging with almost liturgical monotony: keep your voice down, and god damn you. And god damn you too you god damned. Quite suddenly she struck her full glass of planter's punch into his lap and they left the table walking stiffly, their whole bodies fists. [13]

Anyone who has endured a church service of hardly audible, endless repetitions, like a solemn high mass or a litany of the saints, recognizes the aptness of "liturgical monotony." The climaxing metaphor of fists is effective in invoking the couple's bracing embarrassment, their resulting stiffness, and the momentary desire for violent revenge. For his final work, A Death in the Family, Agee was able to bring his gifts of prose to their fullest fruition. Alfred Kazin pays posthumous tribute to his total contribution by writing that it is "the work of a writer whose power with English words can make you gasp."[14]

Agee's achievement with language is the result of a

---

[13]"Six Days at Sea," Fortune, XVI (September, 1937), 117.

[14]Contemporaries (Boston, 1962), p. 187.

rich Southern heritage as well as meticulous craftsmanship.
Ezra Goodman reports that when he succeeded Agee as Time's
film critic, he found in one of the desk drawers a massive
pile of writing paper, on which Agee had endlessly written
and rewritten the opening paragraph of his Hamlet review.
It appeared as though there were some thirty-odd drafts,
with a single word or punctuation mark being changed from
one version to the next.[15] This type of effort by itself,
however, does not produce the results Agee achieved. He
partook of the Southern writer's love of rich, full-flowing
language. He took pride in the rhythm and baroque
sinuosity of that certain form of rhetoric which seems
indigenous to the South. He had, at the top of his form,
both spontaneity and control. A mawkish version of
Pinero's The Enchanted Cottage elicits one of his
typically Southern, flowing responses.

> I can recommend the new Robert Young-
> Dorothy McGuire version to susceptible
> adolescents of any age, but I doubt that
> I can give it--or could now give the old
> one--a fair review, for everything about
> it embarrasses me too painfully for clear
> thought; its solemnly whimsical good
> intentions, its slushy philosophy and
> still slushier dramatizing, the little
> kernels of truth which it turns into so
> much molasses-dipped popcorn, and the
> impressive variety of whimpers, snorts,
> eyedabs, and frantically salvaged sobs
> which it tickled, pleaded, pressed,

---

[15]Goodman, p. 153.

> shanghaied, kicked, clubbed, and above
> all blackmailed out of me. I have no
> objection to tears when they are honest
> ones honestly extracted--quite the
> contrary; and very possibly some of
> these were of that sort, but if so I
> will never know. I had too constantly
> to be pre-occupied with the feeling that
> my spiritual pockets were being picked by
> people with sad sweet smiles who, worse
> still, believed in both the smiles and
> the thieving (156).

Note the repetition of adjectives, nouns, verbs; the length
of the sentences; the frequent parentheses; the direct,
personal note. Southern writers, even the best like
Faulkner or Wolfe, have a tendency to permit the richness
to become too ripe, in that the sentences become strained,
and the meaning deluged by a gush of words. Agee also
falls into these excesses. The first sentence in the
following passage from the review of To Live in Peace is
too concentrated. One sentence cannot comfortably contain
the thought.

> During the long climax these clashings
> blend in such a way that the picture,
> faults and all, soars along one of the
> rarest heights possible to art--the
> height from which it is seen that the
> whole race, including the observer, is
> to be pitied, laughed at, feared for,
> and revered for its delusions of
> personal competence for good, evil, or
> mere survival, as it sleepwalks along
> ground which continuously opens
> bottomless chasms beneath the edges of
> its feet. This seems to me one of the
> truest conceivable perspectives on the
> human predicament (284).

The meaning gets through, but only after tottering near

those bottomless chasms.

Another striking feature of Agee's prose is its poetic quality. The more fully realized type of poetic prose in A Death in the Family is recognizable in the criticism. A facility with metaphorical language not only enriches and elevates the style of a review, but also clarifies the meaning. Condemning the fabricated, insulting myths about death that Hollywood had been foisting on the public for years, Agee terms these practices "as evil as cosmetics on a cadaver" (92). The old Sennett comedies, shown in a movie house with a honky-tonk piano and unpretentious people in the audience, caused laughter "as violent and steady and deafening as standing under a waterfall" (7). A French medieval romance, The Devils Envoys, is said to be beautiful to look at, like "tapestry turned into slow-motion ballet."[16]

A beautifully poetic or evocative sequence in a film is often described in terms equally poetic. Jean Renoir's The Southerner contains a scene which must have evoked Agee's boyhood experiences in the Tennessee Mountains.[17]

---

[16]"Another Time Around," Time, L (September 29, 1947), 98-103.

[17]Cf. the description in The Morning Watch of the young boys' stepping out of chapel into a cold, early morning in the Cumberland mountains. "It was as thrilling cold and as vague and silent here as leaving a hot morning and stepping into a springhouse, and the smell of dead leaves and decaying wood and of the arising year was as keen as the coldness."

"There is a solemnly eager, smoky, foggy 'possum hunt which
may have been studio-faked for all I know; it gets perfectly
the mournful, hungry mysteriousness of a Southern country
winter" (166). "Mournful" and "hungry" are similar, but
the combination with "mysteriousness" is at first striking,
and yet it evokes a lean, sparse, foggy, blurred
countryside. Agee always allowed himself a poetic license
with diction and syntax, particularly notable in his use
of adjectives.

Pauline Kael wonders if Agee was too virtuous to enjoy,
now and then, like the rest of us, a decadent, sleazy,
slick commercial picture. "He didn't very often seem to be
amused by what he was seeing, or to be having much fun."[18]
I vigorously disagree with this opinion. Besides Agee's
relish, at times, of Grade-B movies, his criticism is
stamped with a sense of humor.[19] His laughter is often

---

[18]"That Clean Old Peasant Again," The New Yorker, March 2,
1968, pp. 122-128. As with Renata Adler's complaint about
the debasement of critical language, the irony is that Kael
criticizes Agee for lacking playfulness and humor, the very
qualities she as a critic is most deficient in.

[19]He often, years before the vogue of the auteur theory,
praised the slick work of Raoul Walsh and, on a reviewer's
holiday, would visit the 42nd Street movie houses. On one
such trip, he saw, by pure chance and subsequently praised
in his Nation review, The Curse of the Cat People. Miss
Kael's reference in the same article to "the Christlike
Agee," because of his love only of the pure and simple, is
sadly misinformed.

directed in the form of satire at the exploitation of sex,
and other malpractices of Hollywood. He refers to Lizabeth
Scott as walking through a movie in a manner presumably
intended as alluring, as if "she were lying asleep on a
vertical bed."[20] The Bogart-Bacall sexual fantasy also
amuses him. In To Have and Have Not, Lauren Bacall
represents the kind of derelict sweetheart who is
superficially cool, but inwardly hot as blazes. She seems
even to kiss out of the corner of her mouth (354). Agee's
sense of fun is evident in the review of The Bells of St.
Mary's. Although Ingrid Bergman is well endowed with sex
appeal, she uses considerably too much in portraying
a Mother Superior, and comes embarrassingly close to
"twittering her eyes in scenes with Crosby." Agee then
concludes with the observation that Miss Bergman's
performance in general, "I grieve to say, justifies a
recent piece of radio promotion which rather startlingly
describes a nun: 'Ingrid Bergman has never been lovlier,
hubbahubbahubba'" (185). Surely, Agee was amused by such
nonsense, not offended or embarrassed.

At times, his humor is as cynical and abrasive as the
black humor of the 1960's. As early as 1933, a Fortune
article concerning the Saratoga racing mystique points

---

[20]"The New Pictures," Time, LI (February 16, 1948),
99-101.

towards the darker side of Agee's humor. For many years
the health spas and spring in Saratoga had a predominantly
Jewish clientele. Agee comments, "by way of partial
explanation it may be suggested that Jews, thanks to a
couple of thousand years of Christianity, may be racially
somewhat inclined to hypochondria."[21] In an attack on an
alleged "religious" movie, The Miracle of the Bells, his
repulsion is thinly disguised by the remark that the
picture's box-office gross should be a fair measure of the
depths of American pseudo-religious depravity. Later,
however, he returns to the more usual satirical tone of the
reviews. "The Archangel Michael, familiarly called Mike
throughout the picture, ought to sue."[22]

A box-office ploy which amuses Agee, and which he
treats in a light vein, is Hollywood's "safe fearlessness"
in handling controversial, delicate, or forbidden subjects.
In keeping with Hollywood's genius for deception and
hypocrisy, of which the Code is ample evidence, many
movies of the 1940's brazenly broach and then skirt an
explosive issue. Products such as The Keys of the Kingdom,

---

[21]"August at Saratoga," Fortune, XII (August 1955),
62-69.

[22]"The New Pictures," Time, LI (March 29, 1948), 98-102.

Crossfire and Ride the Pink Horse introduce and then evade
topics such as a priest's potential sexual involvement,
anti-semitism, and the racial prejudices in the South and
Southwest against Negroes and Mexicans. A "daring"
treatment of the dark, irrational forces in Hitchcock's
Spellbound, for which a psychiatric adviser was employed
(with appropriate fanfare and publicity), turns out to be
just so much of the Id as can safely be displayed at
Bergdorf Goodman's (180). The Little Women of World War II,
Tender Comrade, gives a sorority-house treatment to a
serious subject, the death of a soldier. Consequently,
audiences "may feel as if they had been brained with a
a powder puff."[23] Although the humor is too obvious, it
does help to establish the point that instead of being
vicariously immersed in a tragic, common experience for many
families, audiences are not seriously engaged.

Another form of Hollywood deceit Agee enjoys lampooning
is pseudo-sophistication or pretense. Pearl Buck's Dragon
Seed persists in having the Chinese peasants talk in a
manner reminiscent of the Bible, revised by a snappy team
of sixteen Hollywood script-writers. The result:

> This M.G.M. film is a limp-leather-
> bound, goose-fleshy Golden Treasury of
> such talk - 'the wind has brought the

---

[23]"The New Pictures," Time, XLIII (March 27, 1944),
94-96.

> rain' instead of 'it's raining' or just
> watching it fall; 'you place the book
> where my hand cannot reach it' instead
> of 'put that back, damn it' (109).

Because of many such passages throughout the reviews, Manny

Farber is justified in his appreciation of the one

infallibly charming quality of Agee, "an aristocratic

gashouse humor."[24] Agee calls for honesty, simplicity and

truth in films, as Pauline Kael writes, but he also has

fun doing it.

A fierce moral commitment marks Agee's writing as

surely as love, intensity or humor. In reviewing

Shoeshine, he stresses that it is not a defeatist or

despairing work, as some people claimed. He was the only

critic at the time of the film's opening in 1947 to observe

that it is a convincing defense of the ardent and virile

Christian values as well as a pitiful and terrible

demonstration of the effects of their absence or misuse

(279). Agee's basic moral orientation is revealed more

fully in his discussion of the Hollywood Red scare of 1947,

in which ten men were cited for contempt of Congress and

fired by their employers. The conflict is not between

Communism and democracy, but between those who "honor

existence and so, necessarily, morality," and those who do

[24]Farber, pp. 14-15.

not. In Agee's terms, to honor existence is to accept the
burden of responsibility for one's actions. Throughout
his career, he thus equated morality with existence. This
type of ethical substructure, which informs Agee's
criticism, is, as Walter Kerr points out, sadly absent in
the bulk of secular criticism today.[25]

Agee's moral statements are not appendages. They
evolve from a moral consciousness which colors all of his
works. In terms more direct than usually employed in the
reviews, he wrote, in reply to a questionnaire for a
Partisan Review symposium on religion, that the "modern"
conception of sex primarily or exclusively as pleasure
must have done damage as deep and vicious in our age as
the deadliest of the religious attitudes toward sex can
ever have done in former ages.[26] This opinion issues from
the liberal, anti-authoritarian critic who vigorously
advocated a liberalization or outright abolition of the
Code, particularly as it pertained to sex, and who did
not disguise his disgust with the Legion of Decency.

His The Morning Watch is a spiritual autobiography
of the maturing of a young boy, compressed into a few
hours. It is framed in the religious terms and symbols

---

[25]Kerr, p. 13.

[26]"Religion and the Intellectuals," Partisan Review,
XVII (February, 1950), 106-113.

of Good Friday and Easter. "A Mother's Fable" examines,
by means of a tale about elephants, man's relationship to
other men in the light of his ultimate purpose. The most
relentlessly intense work of Agee's is <u>Let Us Now Praise
Famous Men</u>, which Lionel Trilling refers to as one of the
most moral efforts of our American generation,[27] because
of the searing indictment of society, and himself as well,
for allowing so many lives to be ground down into such
abject poverty. Passages like the following, representative of Agee's work as a whole, support Trilling's
judgment. The sharecroppers' graves, of both adults and
children, are described.

> ...and soon, quite soon now, in two
> years, in five, in forty, it will all
> be over, and one by one we shall all
> be drawn into the planet beside one
> another; let us then hope better of
> our children,and of our children's
> children; let us <u>know</u> there is cure,
> there is to be an end to it, whose
> beginnings are long begun, and in slow
> agonies and all deceptions clearing;
> and in the teeth of all hope of cure
> which shall pretend its denial and
> hope of good use to men, let us most
> quietly and in most reverent
> fierceness say, not by its captive
> but by its utmost meanings:
>
> Our father, who art in heaven,
> hallowed be thy name: Thy kingdom
> come ---.[28]

---

[27] E. M. Forster, <u>Aspects of the Novel</u> (New York, 1954),
p. 218.

[28] <u>Let Us Now Praise Famous Men</u> (Boston, 1960), p. 439.

The prose at one point becomes tortured, but more importantly, Agee's fierce compassion and obstinate hope for the Alabama sharecroppers are earnestly communicated.

The major tenet of Agee's moral commitment is humanism. It posits on absolute responsibility for every adult. He rejects as a widely popular excuse, among amateur adherents of Freud's theories, the modern tendency of transferring adult misdeeds to childhood frustrations. It is morally untenable to maintain that an unhappy childhood not only explains but somehow excuses an adult's self-indulgent behavior.[29] Report on Italy, a short film made immediately after the war, contains many shots of "anguished,bewildered human beings, mutely questioning the script's assumption of Italy's all but universal guilt and shame."[30] Instead of accepting the script's assumption, as many in the audience must have, Agee was more concerned with the uncomprehending, vanquished Italian masses. Agee's commitment to his fellow-man was not restricted to theory alone. At a press conference

---

[29]"The New Pictures," Time, XLIX (February 3, 1947), 93-95. Agee rejected much of Freud's teaching; he was not disposed to accept a dimunition of a man's moral responsibility, either for psychological or social reasons.

[30]"Report on Italy," Time, XLV (March 5, 1945), 91-92.

Charlie Chaplin held in New York shortly after the opening
of the poorly received <u>Monsieur Verdoux</u> in 1947, the press
was openly hostile and brow-beat him with questions: was
he a communist, why did he have so little regard for this
country that, after making so much money in it, he was
still a British subject? It is reported that only Agee,
whose control made it possible for him to speak at all, was
able civilly to voice the apologies of some of the
newspaper and magazine reporters when, in effect, he asked
Chaplin what he thought of a country in which a fine
artist, whose pity and concern for the down-trodden had
made him beloved throughout the world, was given the
disgraceful reception just tendered him. Chaplin, smiling
gently, preferred not to discuss that question, but thanked
Agee "very much." In this concrete way, Agee displayed in
public his often stated compassion for other human beings.[31]

R. G. Collingwood states that it is erroneously
believed by the public that a good critic is one who
insists that a society's common magic (which he defines as
that which is designed to bring about a social or

---

[31]Shirley O'Hara, "Chaplin and Hemingway," <u>New Republic</u>,
CXIX (May 5, 1947), 34. This conference undoubtedly was
the beginning of what proved to be, for the remaining
eight years of Agee's life, a deeply felt, mutually
respectful friendship between Chaplin and Agee. Both men
enjoyed many evenings spent together in conversation.

utilitarian result) is also good art.[32] Contrast this with Agee's refusal, for moral reasons, to allow himself during the Second World War to be sucked into the vortex of hysterical, at times inhumane, war propaganda against the Japanese and Germans. He objected to the Army's 1944 Screen Magazine because it contains references to the Japanese as "cockroaches" and "rats," as well as a muted sneer at a Japanese shrine (75). In discussing this whole area of war propaganda in another review, he makes the engaging observation that a victorious nation is prone to act towards defeated enemies in such a way as to damage itself morally to an extent greater than the defeated nation has suffered materially (80).

Agee's countering the popular current or "magic" at that dire time is admirable. Yet, at times, he goes too far. He opposes the newsreels, released to American audiences in May, 1945, which record the Nazi atrocities. The showing, he argues, is an outgrowth of vengeance, which in itself is evil, whether acted upon in hot blood or in a crisis of prevention or, far worse, in the cold-blooded illusion of discharging justice (162). He adds that he did not feel it necessary to see these newsreels. I find this line of reasoning unacceptable. Surely the American people, having lived through four years of war, were

---

[32]Collingwood, p. 93.

entitled to see what had actually occurred during that war,
even the incredibly heinous crimes of the Nazis. The
charge that vengeance was the primary motivating factor for
the showing is also debatable.[33] The admission that he had
no need to see these films personally, and thereby obtain
a more informed judgment, is unworthy of Agee. In this
matter, I believe, his compassion, for even the
perpetrators of some of the most despicable acts in the
history of humanity, obstructed his reason.

It is typical of Agee to admit frankly his doubts,
reservations or even weaknesses, whereas a more aloof
critic would never permit himself such personal revelations.
This complete, honest, yet not intrusive, subjectivity has
played a significant role in establishing Agee's stature
as a critic. An artist in his own right who expended all
of his talents in the criticism, Agee was able to construct
a particular mode of communication between writer and
reader. Creative writing can be defined as communication
through revelation. It is the private Self escaping into

---

[33]Agee might reasonably argue that showing these films
serves no instructive or constructive purpose, since the
crimes were already known, and since pictures of horror
can have little purpose once the horror stops. Yet, there
are many who feel that graphic, painful reminders of man's
inhumanity might provoke into societal involvement the
vast majority of passive, silent, decent people who allow
the few evil men to perpetrate vast crimes. Alain Resnais
in "Night and Fog" displays incredible atrocities for this
reason.

the open. No true writer can long remain incognito.[34]
Agee makes no attempt to remain unknown or, for that
matter, impartial. One critic, in fact, complains that
Agee reacts to films entirely on a gut level. He either
likes a film or he doesn't like it.[35] The charge is
inaccurate, but the relevant question is whether this type
of subjective reaction in a critic is a flaw. Henry James
wrote that nothing would ever take the place of the good
old fashion of "liking" a work of art or not liking it, and
the most advanced criticism would not replace this
"primitive, ultimate test."[36] George Bernard Shaw, like
James, an artist-critic, believed that it is the capacity
for making good or bad art a personal matter that makes a
man a worthy critic.[37] A critic's being subjective, then,
is not, in the estimation of two notable practitioners, a
disqualification.

That Agee is intentionally and consistently a
subjective critic is well documented. In a politically

---

[34]E. B. White and William Strunk, Jr., The Elements of
Style (New York, 1959), p. 53.

[35]Holland, pp. 148-151.

[36]Henry James, "The Art of Fiction," in The House of
Fiction, Essays on the Novel, ed., Leon Edel (London, 1957),
p. 37.

[37]Arlene Croce, "Hollywood the Monolith," Commonweal,
LXIX (January 23, 1959), 430-433.

oriented discussion of Franklin D. Roosevelt, he states
that if there is any excuse for writing so subjectively,
"beyond the fact that I can hardly write or think of
anything else," it is because of political agnosticism.
This parenthetical admission of his subjectivity, intended
only for one particular review, applies equally to his
entire criticism. In the review of Farrebique, Agee
confesses that both the subject and treatment are
obsessions of his. With characteristic forthrightness, he
writes, "so I cannot hope that many other people will be as
deeply excited and satisfied by this film as I am." Yet
because of these obsessions, he adds, any mismanagements
or betrayals of the subject or treatment will be viewed
more mercilessly (296). All of this has the ring of
sincerity, and it would not be unreasonable to assume that
many critics find themselves in similar situations on
occasion, but rarely do they offer this kind of bald
statement of their predilections.

One critic charges that Agee's subjectivity is
inordinate. Revelations of self, although invariably
arresting, continually get in the way of his subject.[38]
Constant intrusions of self, to the point of obscuring
the film under review, are indefensible. With Agee, not

---

[38] _____. Review of Agee on Film: Review and Comments,
New Yorker, XXXIV (December 13, 1958), 215.

only is this not the case, but his subjectivity enhances the reader's understanding of a particular review. Dwight Macdonald maintains that, oddly enough, Agee, by placing himself squarely in the foreground, gives a more truthful picture than the more deliberately objective critic. A reader can allow for Agee's personality as something of a distortion of the picture, but he can not do this with a critic who coolly keeps himself out of the picture and insists that he is presenting not *his* truth but *the* truth.[39]

Though frankly subjective, Agee does maintain a balance between aloof objectivity and intrusive subjectivity. When Alistair Cooke was appointed film critic for the British Broadcasting Corporation in the thirties, he set forth a critic's testament in his first broadcast. He stated that however much in private he might want to rage or protest or moralize, "these actions have nothing to do with criticism." As a moralist, he might be shocked, and as an educator, he might be distressed. But a critic is neither a moralist nor an educator, he is merely a critic, "and I have to try and decide whether Miss Harlow's smiles and pouts were performed expertly enough to entice Mr. Gable away.[40] This

[39]"Agee and the Movies," Film Heritage, III (Fall 1967), 3-11. Macdonald contrasts Agee's subjective method with Truman Capote's allegedly "impersonal" method of reporting in In Cold Blood.

[40]Lindgren, p. 175.

position is obviously and totally different from Agee's
since he often moralizes,rages, and protests in his
criticism. He would reject Cooke's pronouncement as
hollow. At the other extreme, a critic like Pauline
Kael represents a tendency toward an uncontrolled
subjectivity. In reviewing Hud, she disagrees with a
point Bosley Crowther makes that Hud is a social predator,
in that he indulges himself with his neighbor's wife.
This could or could not be true; it is, certainly,
arguable. Yet Miss Kael, to support her rejection of
Crowther's position, offers as evidence the adultery
of her own father: "If Homer, like my father, had
frequented married women or widows..."[41] This type
of personal family revelation seems to be as irrelevant
as it is tasteless. In all of Agee's criticism, and
notwithstanding a compulsive drive toward autobiography
in his fiction, there is no self-exposure or exhibitionism.
His subjectivity seems natural and honest.

One aspect of Agee's subjectivity is, however,
questionable. His belief in simplicity, honesty, and
artlessness in films was transferred to his attitude
toward criticism. He grew to distrust the "professional"
associated with the film industry, and never varied from
the credo set forth in his first article for The Nation.

---

[41]I Lost It at the Movies, pp. 78-79.

"And I will be of use and of interest only in so far as my amateur judgment is sound, stimulating or illuminating" (22). This seems to be a strangely unconvincing position, in that we are not likely to be impressed by a critic or his judgment because he is an amateur. John Updike's admiration for Agee as critic and as writer is discerning, because he refers to this particular flaw. It is not Agee's professionalism that is at fault, but his "blind, despairing belief in an ideal amateurism."[42]

The second concept of Agee's credo can also be questioned, since there are factors more important than a critic's judgment in assessing his over-all worth. Agee's reputation has been increasing since his death in 1955 not because of his amateurism or his particular judgments, but in part because of his sensibility. In this light, W. H. Auden's estimate in 1944 of Agee's reviews far transcending their subject matter is relevant, particularly in view of the quality of the bulk of "Hollywood" products churned out at that time. Lionel Trilling, in another context, describes Agee's sensibility as "so precise, so unremitting, that it is sometimes appalling."[43] A present-day critic pays tribute by writing, "the debt which I, or any other

---

[42]"No Use Talking," New Republic, CXLVII (August 13, 1962), 23-24.

[43]Siegel, p. 13.

young writer who presumes to write about movies, owe to Agee is incalculable." The key, he continues, to Agee's extraordinary achievement lies in his "exacting sensibility," which at times proves "chillingly awesome."[44] Agee's response to Rouquier's Farrebique and Renoir's The Southerner, his reminiscence of comedy's greatest era, his savoring of the work of Jean Vigo and D. W. Griffith all bear testimony to his critical sensibility as finely tuned as it is diverse.

Although Agee's preference in certain areas are on record, he never pontificates or decrees a set of dogmas for the content or style of films. Representative of this flexibility is his treatment , over a span of two years, of the Hollywood journalistic films of the mid-forties, which he heralded, encouraged, cautioned, and finally rejected. Though many of the basic practices in these films were what he was continually calling for, he did not hesitate to dismiss them once they fell into formula. Specifically, he enthusiastically hailed, in March of 1947, the idea embodied in Boomerang: to film a story based on fact, shoot it in an actual town, using actual locations as sets and townspeople as the actors.[45] Since this proved a box-office success, as did the similar 13 Rue Madeleine,

---

[44]loc. cit.

[45]"The New Pictures," Time, XLIX (March 10, 1947), 97-98.

something of a trend developed during the latter part of
the same year. In February, 1948, Agee encouraged this
development, but added that if better documentary-type
movies were to be made, they would have to extend, as well
as transcend, this "journalistic technique."[46] Six months
later, in reviewing The Street Without A Name, he wrote
that semi-documentaries like this were deteriorating into
predictable patterns, and cautioned that if they were to
realize their potentialities, or even stay as effective as
when they had started, they would have to have fresh ideas
and problems.[47] The final note was struck three months
later in Agee's last review written for Time magazine.
Sealed Verdict was dismissed as "a sorry example of
Hollywood's new trick of using authentic buildings to dress
up synthetic stories." Through the realistic settings,
"it is all too easy to spot the old movie corn and the
gimmick."[48] The temptation to defend these films must
have been present, since Agee was one of the first critics
to recognize and broadcast their merits. He therefore
could have associated himself with the trend. This similar

[46]"The New Pictures," Time, LI (February 16, 1948),99-
101.

[47]"Relative Anonymity," Time,LII (August 9, 1948), 74-78.

[48]"The New Pictures," Time, LII (November 8, 1948), 102-
106.

temptation has proven too great for some critics who,
having in part helped to create a trend, adamantly argue
for its merits long after the original energy and impetus
have been dissipated. Andrew Sarris with the "auteur"
theory is a current example.

On more than one occasion, Agee displays the courage
to alter or transcend his own principles. One of the
movements with which he is most closely associated is
Italian neo-realism. His laudatory review of Open City,
the first of the neo-realist films to be seen in this
country, was followed by even greater praise for Sunshine.
Luigi Zampa's To Live In Peace similarly received high
commendation. Some three years after the success of Open
City, Agee thoroughly rejected the Italian Furia, a story
of rural adultery which has all of the neo-realist
trappings. At best, it is an earnest attempt, "but
overrated by those who think that the Italians can do no
wrong."[49] Similar is his reaction to Alfred Hitchcock's
The Rope, a film which in theory violates many of the
principles Agee espouses: a sense of motion, a visual
aliveness, the use of real locations, the use of non-
professional actors, simple yet effective editing. In
contrast, the film boasts a cast of professional actors,

[49]"Cast of Characters," Time, LI (March 1, 1958), 84-89.

has not a single cut, and was shot in one studio set in solid ten minute reels, with the end of each reel dissolving into the beginning of the next. Agee's reaction is that "Director Hitchcock brought off a tour de force---Continuous action builds a tension all its own."[50] This does not denote a lack of principles or even a disdain of consistency, but an open mind and the confidence to be flexible. Agee's criticism offers concrete evidence of Edward Fischer's sensible theory that it is hazardous for a critic to align himself too fully with one artistic style because it may blind him to the virtues in others. A critic may prefer one style, but he should never forget that "art wears many faces."[51] For this reason, Pauline Kael with validity can write, "the greatness of critics like Bazin in France and Agee in America may have something to do with their using their full range of intelligence and intuition, rather than relying on formulas."[52]

Agee allows his flexibility at times to lapse into

---

[50]"The New Pictures," Time, LI (September 13, 1948), 102-106.

[51]Fischer, 75.

[52]I Lost It at the Movies, pp. 266-267.

vagueness. The first half of his review of Orson Welles'
The Stranger is a frank, subjective exposition of Agee's
generally negative feelings, past and present, in relation
to Welles. As a preface to an analysis of the film itself,
this is not only acceptable, but could serve to clarify
the meaning of the review. In this case, only antitheses
and generalized remarks follow. The film is not
adventurous, yet it is not self-indulgent; it is not
important or new, yet it is not pretentious or arty. He
does call it "more graceful, intelligent, and enjoyable
than most other movies." Not one concrete reference to
anything in the film is made to substantiate this broad
claim. The most nearly specific line in the review only
serves to confound further. Agee refers to the atmosphere
by declaring that "although I have occasionally seen
atmospheres used in films in far grander poetic context, I
don't think I have seen them more pleasantly and expertly
appreciated" (205). This type of remark raises more
questions than it answers. Does this mean, then, that the
use of atmospheres in this film is poetic, or just pleasant
and appreciated? What visible effect on the film is there,
if any, of the film-makers' expertly appreciating the
atmospheres employed? Since the editors of The Nation
permitted Agee complete freedom, this ambiguity was not
caused by editorial cutting. This vagueness is
unsettlingly similar to the last line of a review of the

spy-counterspy story <u>The House on 92nd Street</u>.
"Unpersuasive, often skilled, generally enjoyable" (177).
That one ordinarily does not enjoy a detective-type story
unless it is persuasive and convincing is axiomatic. Also
one wonders why, if it is skillfully made, is it not
persuasive. Prior to this closing line, Agee praises the
actors for "effective pseudo-naturalistic performances,"
but later adds that by the way they look and act, they
could be detected by anyone interested "at five hundred
paces." What, precisely, does Agee mean by effective
performances, since in the detective story genre
performances are judged according to the degree of
plausibility the actors can impart to the characters they
are portraying?

In sum, Agee's flexibility is a critical asset, since
he is perceptive enough and secure enough from dogmas to
appreciate the complexity involved in understanding.
R. G. Collingwood points out that in any act of cognition,
many phases of understanding are involved, each complete
within itself and each leading on to the next. The doctrine
of a plurality of meanings expounded by Thomas Aquinas in
relation to the interpretation of scripture applies equally
to the interpretation of literature - or film.[53]

---

[53]Collingwood, p. 311.

Agee is able to grasp the fact that seldom is there only one correct interpretation, whether it be of a film or of a passage in scripture. At times, however, his critical openness collapses into vague, ambiguous generalizations.

The occasional failings do not justify John Simon's charge that Agee was scrupulous, forced to see the other side of every view, every statement, every sentence, "even as he was writing."[54] Agee does appear disconcertingly ambivalent in certain reviews, but upon close examination the seeming contradictions can be explained. His final paragraph of the first-part review of The Best Years of Our Lives is, in itself, puzzling. It is possible, he states, to call the whole picture one long pious deceit, and it is obligatory to observe that what could have been done perfectly "was murdered in the cradle" or reduced to a grade-school level. Agee concludes with, "Yet, I feel a hundred times more liking and admiration for the film than distaste or disappointment" (231). Having specified the film's weaknesses, particularly its failure to realize its potential, he analyzes its achievements: the script provides for an open, visually oriented film, the photography by Toland is the finest in any American movie since Greed, and the direction by William Wyler is warm and direct, without any emotional excesses or mannerisms.

---

[54]"Exemplary Failure," The New York Times Book Review, August 14, 1966, p. 2.

To be pleased and disappointed at the same time, to feel
both deeply, and to be able to articulate both reactions in
detail is critical flexibility and acuity, not
scrupulousness.

Agee's critical judgment has withstood the test of
time, even with shortcomings. An intuitive perceptivity
infuses much of the criticism. Consistent with his primary
interest in character, Agee's insights into the behaviour
and inter-actions of people are often brilliant. In The
Best Years of Our Lives veterans keep meeting each other
at a friendly bar. Agee submits that once servicemen of
such disparate classes as the three in the picture became
civilians, they would rarely meet, and if they did, it
would be with more embarrassment than with friendliness
(230). In The Treasure of the Sierra Madre, the intruder
is killed by bandits, and the three prospectors, who were
a short time before ready to kill this man themselves,
approach to identify the dead body.

> Bogart, the would-be-tough guy, cocks
> one foot upon a rock and tries to look
> at the corpse as casually as if it were
> fresh-killed game. Tim Holt, the
> essentially decent young man, comes
> past behind him and, innocent and unaware
> of it, clasps his hands as he looks down,
> in the respectful manner of a boy who
> used to go to church. Walter Huston, the
> experienced old man, steps quietly
> behind both, leans to the dead man as
> professionally as a doctor to a patient
> and gently rifles him for papers (329).

This analysis takes into account the characters' previous
actions and attitudes, and the specificity of insight Agee
brings to his understanding of the scene is striking. The
scene itself includes no lingering or telling close-ups, and
is only a few seconds long. Few viewers, critics or laymen,
would "see" so much in such a brief scene, even with
repeated viewings.

At the end of the war documentary "The Battle of San
Pietro," the camera moves along a line of children and
babies, while the commentator tersely states that in a short
time, they will have forgotten the war. The camera then
pans in silence a heart-rending scene of total disaster.
Agee writes that at this point in the film the commentator's
remark is not the optimistic inanity it first appears to be,
since these children, forgetting, are unwittingly preparing
themselves as fodder for the next war (328). Watching with
horror and pity the children ravaged by war, one would
probably wonder upon hearing the commentator's remark, how
they, in the face of such agony, could ever forget, and yet
the realization comes that they probably will forget. The
commentator's remark, then, has meaning and irony in itself.
Agee, however, perceives another layer of irony and
significance.

Since, as McLuhan and others have pointed out, the
content of any new medium is always the content of the
older medium, Agee had a host of occasions to render

judgments on literary topics. Olivier's film treatment of
Henry V, acclaimed a work of art, yet has flaws. The
comics fail to give the narration of Falstaff's death any
of "the dizzying blend of comedy and noble piteousness it
has in the text" (208). Agee in this apt phrase is able
to capture, unlike the film, the essence of one of the
finer scenes in the play. Years earlier, in a letter to
Father Flye, he revealed similarly discerning judgment.
Concerning the writing style of Theodore Dreiser, he
declared, "Dreiser's English is bum, yet it has a peculiar
beauty and excellence. You feel you're reading a rather
inadequate translation of a very foreign novel--Russian
probably."[55] Agee's literary judgment, however, has one
notable blind spot. For reasons never specified, he does
not appreciate Eugene O'Neill, numbered among this
country's greatest playwrights. The following summation
of The Iceman Cometh is typical of Agee's response to
O'Neill. The ideal audience would be some "non-temperance
Old Men's Home along the Bowery--it is in that sense a
genuine and likeable folk-play" (276). This niggardly,
sarcastic appraisal is entirely dwarfed by the stature the
play has since justly achieved in dramatic literature.
The honored trilogy Mourning Becomes Electra is dismissed

---

[55]Letters of James Agee to Father Flye, p. 25.

as a travesty of Freudian psychology and a near-parody of
Greek tragedy (381). I suspect that Agee's rejection of
O'Neill rests on a love of language and a dislike of Freud.
Agee enjoyed Dreiser's "bum" English because it has a
peculiar beauty and excellence. O'Neill's language, often
crude and heavy, is to a large extent devoid of poetry.
Further, O'Neill's fascination and theatrical experiments
with Freud's theories probably were hard for Agee to take.

Agee arduously argues that historically based films
should be faithful to the history involved. For such a
perceptive, literate critic, one is puzzled by his stubborn
insistence on this point. In a 1936 letter, he set forth
his writer's credo as attempting to arrive as near truth
and whole truth as humanly possible, and presenting this
as clearly and cleanly as possible.[56] This concern for
truth, along with honesty and simplicity, is everywhere
present in the criticism. Yet his working definition of
truth, "spiritual life, integrity and growth" is not
synonymous with strict historical accuracy. <u>Wilson</u>, for
instance, is disappointing because much of it is
"fictional invention." The finest scene in the film,
Wilson's terrifying outburst against Germany's Ambassador

---

[56]Ibid., pp. 76-77.

Bernstorff, is weakened because it is "wholly fictional."[57]
He also insists on counterpointing every historical
inaccuracy in Roger Touhy, Gangster with a revelation of
historical fact. Ironically, some twenty years later, the
regular Time reviewer dismissed Bonnie and Clyde, another
historically based gangster film, because of its historical
inaccuracies. Months later, Stefan Kanter, in a brilliant
Time cover story on Arthur Penn's Bonnie and Clyde, had
enough fortitude and integrity to reject outright his
colleague's prior review of the film. "Time's review made
the mistake of comparing the fictional and real Bonnie and
Clyde, a totally irrelevant exercise."[58]

Agee persisted throughout his tenure as critic in this
exercise in irrelevancy. It seems strange that Agee
ignored the lessons of the masters, notably Shakespeare,
who molded history into dramatic patterns for artistic,
at times didactic, but not historical purposes. Agee's
insistence on historical accuracy may be understood in part
by his love for order and precision as a writer, which
results in an unusually observant care with details, both

---

[57]"Wilson," Time, XLIV (August 7, 1944), 84-86. His
judgment on the film as a whole is valid. Now more than
in 1944, it does seem to be little more than a postured
type of magazine illustration.

[58]Stefan Kanter, "The Shock of Freedom in Films," Time
(December 8, 1967) 66-76.

in his fiction and criticism. In writing The Morning
Watch, set in his old school of St. Andrew's in Tennessee,
he wrote to Fr. Flye for the exact time the sun sets on
particular dates in that locale. Any explanation does not
excuse Agee's untypical literalness in this one area, since
as Edward Fischer aptly writes,the "patch of history" is
insignificant compared to the artist's focus on individuals.
"All great fiction is primarily about individuals."[59]
Agee's demand for historical accuracy may go far in
explaining his least exciting, most plodding film script,
Noa-Noa. His remaining scrupulously faithful to Gauguin's
life and spirit, and frequently quoting from his diary,
imparted no creative charge to the never-produced script.
It appears that the facts, records, and diaries of Gauguin
assumed a commanding importance. This aesthetic principle,
then, impaired not only his criticism when he was dealing
with historical movies, but his own scenario based on
recorded fact.

In an over-all assessment, however, Agee's judgment
is sound. Theodore Strauss, Agee's senior editor at Time,
believes that with all of the dazzling writing, he missed
the point completely as to a film's vitality or lack of
it.[60] Though a decidedly minority view, it raises the

---

[59]Fischer, p. 19.
[60]Goodman, p. 153.

question of whether Agee is too much form and too little substance. In the majority of major reviews, those in which a full column or more is devoted to one film, his opinions have been supported by the test of time. Agee's immediate acceptance in 1947 of da Sica's Shoeshine as one of the rarest things in contemporary art, a true tragedy, has been confirmed by a host of critics over the past twenty years.[61] Agee's enthusiastic endorsement in 1948 of Huston's The Treasure of the Sierra Madre has similarly been corroborated by its stature today as one of the finest American films of its kind.[62] Huston's now-celebrated "The Battle of San Pietro," kept in constant circulation among schools, art houses, and festivals, was hailed by Agee in 1945 as the outstanding factual film of the Second World War (186). Olivier's productions of Henry V and Hamlet also were judged initially to be great works of art, and they are so considered today by a majority of critics and film-goers. Agee's tempered acceptance of the following three films as flawed, minor masterpieces likewise has proven accurate: Dreyer's Day of Wrath, Eisenstein's Ivan the Terrible, and

---

[61]Kael, I Lost It at the Movies, p. 102. Miss Kael terms it one of the rare works of art in film.

[62]Hollis Alpert, "Offbeat Director in Outer Space," The New York Times, January 16, 1966, p. 14. Stanley Kauffmann also rates The Treasure of the Sierra Madre as one of the best American movies ever made.

Wilder's <u>Sunset Boulevard</u>. Jonathan Harker, in a statement which is representative of many other film critics, writes that Agee's judgment is not impeccable, seen with the hindsight of fifteen years, it is only "incomparably the best of his period."[63]

Aligned with his celebration of the emerging art of the film, Agee, however, has a tendency to over-praise films. All of the New York critics, from John Mason Brown and Manny Farber to John McCarten and Bosley Crowther, warmly greeted the fresh, vigorous air of Rossellini's <u>Open City</u> in 1946. Agee also understandably over-reacted to America's first encounter with Italian neo-realism. The film, viewed in historical perspective, can now be placed in context: it was a welcome relief from the bulk of Hollywood glossy products of that era. Compared to films of the 1960's, however, its impact palls, and it is remembered today as a film of historical interest rather than, as Agee extravagantly termed it, a film that can be ranked with the works of Eisenstein, Dovzhenko, Pudovkin, and among some of the greatest works of art of this century (195). None of the other critics went to this extreme in commending <u>Open City</u>. Chaplin's <u>Monsieur Verdoux</u> is another film, copiously praised by Agee in a

[63]Review of <u>Agee on Film: Reviews and Comments</u>, <u>Film Quarterly</u>, XII (Spring 1959), 58-61.

three-part <u>Nation</u> review, which at present is more important as a Chaplin work than as a great film in its own right. It seems probable that in this one instance Agee was moved to such staunch praise for personal and political reasons rather than for purely aesthetic ones. Dwight Macdonald makes essentially this point after contrasting his negative review written subsequent to a 1964 showing of the film, with Agee's 1947 review.[64]

Agee as a critic is literally generous to a fault. William Wellman's <u>The Story of G.I. Joe</u> as a war film compares favorably to the pulp that passed for fictional war films of the mid-forties. Samuel Fuller, one of the gods of the underground cinema mainly because of his achievements in directing war movies, acknowledged recently how adolescent and completely insincere most war films are, with an occasional exception like <u>The Story of G.I. Joe</u>.[65] This kind of tempered praise is what the film deserves. Agee, however, extolls it excessively. He compares it with

[64]"Chaplin, Verdoux or Agee," <u>Esquire</u>, Vol.63, (April 1965), 19. One conjectures that the press conference which was shockingly rude to Chaplin after the premiere of <u>Monsieur Verdoux</u>, and at which Agee defended Chaplin, might be a strong personal reason for Agee to go to such inordinate lengths to praise the film.

[65]"The Issue," <u>Film: Book 2, Films of Peace and War</u>, ed. Robert Hughes (New York, 1962), p. 165.

the great war poetry of Walt Whitman and the memorable
Civil War photographs of Matthew Brady (173). Farrebique
is today appreciated as a respectable achievement in the
very limited genre of nature films. It received an
ecstatic reception from Agee, although he prefaced it with
an admission of his being obsessed with the particular
subject treated (296-299). The Curse of the Cat People now
seems stilted, dated, and at best no more than what its
director Val Lewton probably intended it to be, a good
Grade B horror movie. Agee in 1944 hailed it as one of the
finest fiction films of the year, "consistently alive,
limber, poetic, humane" (137). The Bank Dick, at best a
rickety though funny vehicle for W. C. Fields, is ranked
among the best movies ever made.

There are, conversely, only a few instances where
Agee condemns films generally considered worthy. He
devotes only one-quarter of a Nation column to David Lean's
Brief Encounter, paying the back-handed compliment of
classifying it a splendid example of "women's magazine
fiction." Relatively "dinky and sentimental," it is a neat
lesson in packaged realism, that which can be accommodated
comfortably in a lady's handbag (235). This judgment has
been proven not only harsh but also unjust by the film's
continued and deserved appreciation. Indeed, it is

frequently mentioned as one of Lean's finer achievements.[66]
Another film unfavorably reviewed by Agee is William
Wellman's The Ox-Bow Incident. He correctly exposes some
of the self-conscious artistry, like the gnarled lynching
tree. Completely missed, however, is the film's power,
generated through adroit handling of character and
situation, particularly Wellman's building to the closing
scene, not even mentioned in Agee's review. For these as
well as other reasons, the film over the years has
achieved a deservedly respectable position in the history
of American movies.

To establish the fallibility of Agee's judgment is
not to disqualify him as a critic. More than any other
American film critic, he has contributed to the film's
acceptance, in the 1950's and 1960's, as an art form.
Raymond Spottiswoode writes that criticism at its best
can provide an opportunity for, rather than directly

---

[66]Roger Manvell, The Film and the Public (Baltimore,
1955), p. 156. Agee's comment as to the film's being
sentimental is not unjust. The story does depend upon a
sentimentalization of the romance, like the eating scene
in the railroad station's lunch room when the characters
are first falling in love. Yet the film deserves more
than a one-quarter column dismissal. The farewell scene
is memorable: in the same lunch room, with the two lovers
wanting to say so much to each other before the train
comes, an intrusive, distracting bore of an old-lady
friend gratingly chatters on and on. Lean's deft
directorial touches like this one make the movie worthy
of respect.

causing, good art to flourish. Enlightened criticism can be the soil and sun, but never the life of the plant.[67] In this sense, Agee has influenced, not directly caused, some of the modern trends in the production of movies. Some current critics, like Joel Siegel, publicly acknowledge this debt. Others continue to support many of Agee's basic positions. Pauline Kael, for example, attacks with relish, exactly as Agee did, Hollywood's policy of "safe fearlessness" in presenting, then dodging, controversial topics. She even ridicules the same types of hypocrisy: in a movie attack on capital punishment, the person sentenced to death cannot be guilty; in a race relation movie, the Negroes and Jews who are mistreated by sadists and bullies are transcendent heroes, scarcely recognizable as ordinary mortals.[68] In discussing Crossfire, she asks what if the Jew who was murdered was a draft-dodger or a conscientious objector, instead of being, once again, the liberal stereotype and a decorated war hero.[69]

More significantly, however, Agee had much to do with helping to prepare the audience which today attends the

---

[67]Spottiswoode, p. 314.

[68]I lost It at the Movies, p. 142.

[69]"Movies, the Desperate Art," Film: An Anthology, ed. Dan Talbot (New York, 1959), p. 200.

expanding number of revival houses, art theatres, and film
festivals. He did this principally by specifying his
appreciation of what the more adventurous directors
attempted. Occasionally, he encouraged an admirable
attempt, such as Warner Brothers' Possessed. This story
of a dazed derelict, suffering a form of schizophrenia,
is noted for its effective uses of sound: distorted
musical flashbacks, exaggerated rain, amplified heartbeats.
The attempt, assumed at the risk of confusing audiences, to
convey the heroine's split sense of reality is even more
highly commended. Agee concludes that other film-makers
should take more risks on this order, since the results are
much more exciting than confusing (373). Roman Polanski's
Repulsion and Ingmar Bergman's Persona are two recent,
perplexing though fascinating, studies in this area of the
abnormal.

Agee is at his best in detailing the work of one of
the masters. Typical is this response to Jean Vigo's
"Zero de Conduite" and L'Atalante, written in 1947 some
fifteen years prior to the achievements of Resnais, Fellini,
Antonioni, Varda, and others.

> As I see it the trick is, simply, that
> Vigo gets deeper inside his characters
> than most people have tried on film, is
> not worried about transitions between
> objective, subjective, fantastic, and
> sub-conscious reality, and mixes as many
> styles and camera tricks, as abruptly,
> as he sees fit--always so far as I can
> see, using the right style at the right

> moment, and always using it with force,
> charm, and originality. I assume that
> he intended, as one of his main points,
> to insist that these several levels of
> reality are equal in value, and
> interpenetrative; and I would accept this
> aesthetically for its enrichment of
> poetic perception, metaphor, and device,
> even if I rejected it intellectually (263).

The differentiated consciousness in Resnais' Last Year at
Marienbad and Muriel, the fluid shifts between objective
and subjective reality in Fellini's 8½ and Juliet of the
Spirits, the merging of reality and illusion in Antonioni's
Blow-up, the fantasy insets of Agnes Varda's Le Bonheur all
demonstrate that what Agee once hailed as courageously
creative has now become a basic part of contemporary film
grammar.

A heightened realism, brought about by the fusion of
fictional and documentary films, also has become an
established mode. Agee in the 1940's employed the term
poetic realism to embody many of the now current practices.
In France, The New Wave uses actual backgrounds, and the
more recent cinema verite insists on "real" heroes (non-
professional actors) and hand-held cameras. In Britain,
the vogue is new realism, with its simple plots concerning
ordinary people, and the use of actual locations. In the
United States what has been termed "direct cinema" of the
1960's prefers honesty and simplicity. These various
developments rely on a documentary approach with a focus
on plausible human beings. These distinguishing features

are the very ones that Agee encouraged and praised whenever
he had the opportunity. Furthermore, the 1966 Film
Festival in Lincoln Center made clear that directors are
now free from bondage to literature. No longer do they
follow the rules of the drama or novel. Their rich visual
vocabularies declare that they mean "to write with their
lens and not with their pens."[70] Agee over the years
advocated a visually oriented cinema, free from the
dominance of print. He realized that the film would not
emerge as a serious, independent art form while it
subserved literary forms.

One of the most recent as well as most satisfying
movements is the new Czechoslovak cinema. Films like Jan
Kadar's The Shop on Main Street, Jiri Menzel's Closely
Watched Trains, Ivan Passer's Intimate Lighting, and Milos
Forman's Loves of a Blond have all received international
critical and popular acclaim. These films represent in
content and technique what Agee most admired. They
achieve a sensitive, simple portrayal of, in the words of
Passer, "life as it is, unheroic, unexceptional but
nonetheless interesting."[71] In the humanist tradition of
Renoir, da Sica, and Vigo, they observe small human
aspirations in terms of a gentle, never heavy poignancy or

[70] _____, "The Eyes Have It," Time, (September 23, 1966),
p. 74.

[71] loc. cit.

a type of quiet tragi-comedy. Milos Forman, who
acknowledges his debt to the Italian neo-realists, works
with a careful balance of professional actors and
handpicked amateurs, and uses actual locations as well as
the other advantages of a documentary approach in directing
his original scripts, which appeal mainly to the eyes.[72]
This Czech development is the most complete realization to
date of Agee's desire for poetic realism, the style he
believed to be best suited to the film medium. As with
the other modern trends in cinema, it is more than
coincidence that the principles for which Agee most
vigorously argued have become widely accepted. Agee did
not cause these trends, but his film criticism, which has
been increasing in stature on both sides of the Atlantic
in the past two decades, has exerted some influence on the
young directors.

One of the distinguishing marks of Agee as a critic
is his creativity. He often transcends the ordinary
critic's analysis of a film's strengths and weaknesses to
conceptualize in detail what this work might have achieved.
In one review he openly admits to making certain
suggestions jealously, "because I would so love to make
the films rather than see them made" (133). This desire

---

[72]Jan Zalman, "Question Marks on the New Czechoslovak
Cinema," Film Quarterly, XXI (Winter 1967-68), 18-27.

to make and direct films caused Agee, in the words of
Dwight Macdonald, to be a "frustrated director."[73] Agee's
frustration reached its peak in the writing of Noa-Noa,
which director Jospeh Mankiewicz has labelled the most
complete blueprint for a film ever written. It is so
thoroughly detailed, it could be shot without an original
word of the director.[74]

Agee's desire to direct was not a result of his writing
film critiques. At the age of twenty-one, he revealed two
strong ambitions, composing music and directing movies of
his own authorship.[75] In an unpublished letter to Father
Flye, dated February 24, 1925, Agee at the age of sixteen
indicated the same directorial orientation, the tendency
to see a film from the inside, from the maker's viewpoint.
He exuberantly announced that he had seen a truly great
movie, referred to as Frank Norris' McTeague instead of
Erich von Stroheim's adaptation of the novel, which he
entitled Greed. He literally raved about the unnamed
German director's ability to create a brand of realism,
which, in the vernacular of a sixteen-year old, made all

---

[73]Against the American Grain, (New York, 1962), p. 154.

[74]Richard Culahan, "A Cult Grew Around a Many-Sided
Writer," Life, LV (November 1, 1963), 69-72.

[75]The Letters of James Agee to Father Flye, p. 40.

of the other movies he had seen up to that point, "not
worth thirty cents,"[76] Father Flye, when asked why Agee
never directed films, replied that he had always wanted to
be a director, but the opportunity never presented itself.

Agee's ability to project the specific possibilities
of the medium, in relation to a particular film under
review, elevates his criticism.[77] He is always alert to
what might have been. Reviewing The Human Comedy, he
voices annoyance with the neglect of opportunities which
would be only too evident to filmmakers with more cinematic
sense. In one sequence, a young child hears a freight
train coming, runs up close to it, waves, and is answered
by a singing Negro. With any imagination about the
viewpoint of the child, Agee writes, this "could have been
a roaring and miraculous half-minute." Instead, not one
advantage is taken, and, to make the scene close to
shameful, the Negro has the "fruity vibrato" of a

---

[76]Information obtained during an interview with Father
Flye on January 9, 1968, in New York City.

[77]Many critical theorists would disagree, arguing, in the
tradition of Coleridge, that a critic should judge only
what was attempted, not what could or should have been
attempted. As long as the critic, as Agee did, exercises
restraint,not making this unorthodox practice the substance
of his criticism, I think it can impart imagination and
excitement to that criticism.

professional singer (32). In <u>Street of Chance</u>, the
audience shares the protagonist's amnesia only to the
extent of making one discovery at a time. Agee points out
that under this condition, the audience could have been
made to live through the experience of seeing not only
people but streets, windows, even noises, like the sound of
an automobile starting, posing as cryptic threats.[78] For
another work of untapped potential, <u>National Velvet</u>, Agee
provides an outline for what appears to be a far superior
film. In the race scene, the chance for a sharply pointed
study of an inexperienced, frightened girl competing with
tough and seasoned jockeys is forfeited "for the sake of a
few minutes of conventional spills and mass galumphing."[79]
The prior sequence of the horse in preparation for the race
is another reduction to generalized pretty pictures,
instead of being a précis of the pure, technical detail
which must have thrilled, informed, and intensified the
girl and should have done the same for the audience (134).

At times, however, Agee's desire for direction leads
to distortion. In analyzing <u>The Lost Weekend</u>, he makes
such unreasonable demands on the film-makers that an
erroneous impression results.

---

[78]"Street of Chance," <u>Time</u>, XL (December 21, 1942), 100.

[79]"The New Pictures," <u>Time</u>, XLIV (December 25, 1944),
44-48.

> There is very little appreciation, for
> instance, of the many and subtle moods
> possible in drunkenness; almost no
> registration of the several minds inside
> a drinker's brain; hardly a trace of the
> narcissism and self-deceit which are so
> indispensable or of the self-loathing and
> self-pity which are so invariable; hardly
> a hint, except through abrupt action, of
> the desperation of thirst (183).

This detailing of the lost, but possible, opportunities
excites a vision of a brilliant film. Some eight years
after writing this, Agee realized one of his finest
character studies in Ralph, the self-pitying, self-loathing,
desperate drunk of A Death in the Family. The foregoing
passage, however, implies that director Billy Wilder offers
only the meagerest hints and traces of an alcoholic's
plight. This is not true. Self loathing is sufficiently,
though not brilliantly, treated in the latter scenes between
Ray Milland and Jane Wyman, particularly his reactions to
her insistent faith in him. Self-pity is clearly revealed
in the bar scene in which Milland recounts to the bartender
the story of his meeting with Miss Wyman. Something near
the full force, rather than a hint, of desperation is
communicated by Milland's search for his hidden bottle
and his subsequent rationing and measuring of the liquor.

In this review, the artist dominated the critic.
Since this seldom happened, though, the criticism is
enriched by Agee's extraordinary dual role of critic-
creator. As part creator, Agee is less inhibited than

other film reviewers in freely allowing his subjective, intense, sensitive personality to come through in the reviews. Over a period of eight years, Agee proved to be an artist-critic, responsible for the most original and imaginative film criticism America has yet produced.

AFTERWORD

It has been fashionable in some literary circles to debate whether Agee, having died at the relatively early age of forty-five, would have fulfilled his promise if he had lived a fuller life, or whether his source of creativity had, in large part, diminished before the time of his death. The question is academic. The relevant point is that he made an individual and a significant contribution, even with a relatively small body of work. His position in the twentieth century, as a minor figure with a major talent, is secure. To date, there have been three doctoral dissertations, scattered articles, and a few chapters written on Agee. The dissertations have consisted of a critical survey of his major works; a treatment of his relation to mass culture; and an examination of his film criticism.[1] It seems to me that a few studies on Agee yet remain to be undertaken.

A topic only touched upon in the present work is the relation between Agee's criticism and his fiction. His reverence for reality is well-documented in the criticism. How faithful was he to this ideal in his own creative writings? Is there a significant difference in the commitment to "reality" in his Hollywood film scripts of the 1950's and in his 1939 Let Us Now Praise Famous Men? Agee is also

---

[1]
The critical survey of his major works, "James Agee: A Critical Study," a dissertation by Peter Hakan Ohlin at the University of New Mexico, was published under the title Agee in New York by Ivan Obolensky, Inc., in 1966.

constant in demanding simplicity, honesty, and purity. These exacting criteria could be applied to his own fiction.

A related topic would be of a more psychological nature. What happens to the artist who becomes a critic? In what ways, and with what relevance, did the dual function of artist-critic affect Agee's works? It is possible to trace his evolution, beginning at Harvard, where he did both critical and creative writing to his years after graduation, during which he wrote no criticism, to his assignment with _Time_ in 1939 as book reviewer. After eight years as a critic, he devoted his remaining seven years to creative efforts, with only occasional critical pieces. From a textual explication of certain works written at specific times, it may be possible to better understand the creative and critical faculties, and their interactions.

There is a need for an interpretive biography of Agee as a prototype of the modern, restless artist in search of his art. No one muse could sufficiently hold him. He alternated constantly between critical and creative writing, and he switched from one medium to another, from one genre to another. He worked in the film, writing both television and movie scenarios, and spent some fifteen years in the field of journalism. Throughout his career he wrote poetry, a novella, a novel, short stories, essays, and intense, memorable letters. This restlessness was paralleled in his personal life: countless employers, three marriages, many homes. What is reflected in this frenetic search? Is Agee an image of the self-destructive urge in an artist, or is he the image, in John Simon's estimation, of an exemplary failure?

Other possible areas of study are more focused. W. H. Auden believes that Agee belongs in the most select class of journalists of the twentieth century. Both John Updike and Alfred Kazin think that Agee was well suited to journalism, since he needed the pressure, discipline, and confinements of journalistic writing. Dwight Macdonald, on the other hand, feels that Agee squandered his talents for the Luce empire. From his days as editor of the Harvard Advocate, there is no disputing that he was attracted by this type of writing. A study would evaluate what effects the demands and pressures of this field had on his literary efforts and would assess his particular strengths and weaknesses as a journalist. Seldom has a literary figure been so involved, over such an extended period, in journalism.

Tangential to this study would be an examination of Agee's years in Hollywood. No work has been undertaken to guage the effects on the literary writer who, like F. Scott Fitzgerald or Nathanael West, becomes a part of the Hollywood system. What are the results of the collaboration of Agee, first with John Huston (The African Queen), and then with Charles Laughton (The Night of the Hunter)? Why did Agee, who was so clearly opposed to film adaptations while a critic, spend most of his energy adapting literary works for the screen? Was Hollywood inevitable, after his career in the commercial world of journalism? His finest work, A Death in the Family, was written during the Hollywood years. There are many questions to be answered concerning this period, and a few scripts, like White Mane, Green Magic, and The Quiet One, deserve more than the scant attention they have received.

For the most part, these proposed studies of Agee would examine
not only the works themselves, but also the circumstances surrounding
their origins.

BIBLIOGRAPHY

I. PRIMARY SOURCES

A. Books by James Agee

Agee on Film: Reviews and Comments. New York, McDowell
        Obolensky, 1958.

Agee on Film, Vol. II: Five Film Scripts. New York,
        McDowell Obolensky, 1960.

A Death in the Family. New York, McDowell Obolensky, 1957.

The Letters of James Agee to Father Flye. New York,
        George Braziller, 1962.

Let Us Now Praise Famous Men. Boston, Houghton Mifflin
        Co., 1941. Reprinted in 1960.

The Morning Watch. Boston, Houghton Mifflin Co., 1951.

Permit Me Voyage. New Haven, Yale University Press, 1934.

A Way of Seeing. New York, Viking, 1965.

B. Reviews, Articles, and Short Stories

"Also Showing," Time, LI (June 7, 1948), 98-102.

"Another Time Around," Time, L (September 29, 1947), 96-103.

"Artic Passage," Time, XLII (September 27, 1943), 97.

"August in Saratoga," Fortune, VIII (August 1935), 62-69.

"Bewitched," Time, XLVI (September 3, 1945), 91-92.

"Boos & Bravos," Time, XLVII (April 1, 1946), 93-96.

"Cast of Characters," Time, LI (March 1, 1958), 84-89.

"Documentaries Grow Up," Time, XLII (September 13, 1943),
        94-95.

"Farrebique," Time, LI (March 15, 1948), 100-104.

"The Fighting Lady," Time, XLV (January 22, 1945), 91-92.

"The Forest Rangers," Time, XL (November 2, 1942), 97.

"For Whom the Bell Tolls," _Time_, XLII (August 2, 1943), 55-60.

"Frenchmen's Creek," _Time_, XLIV (October 9, 1944), 94-96.

"Great Expectations," _Time_, XLIX (May 26, 1947), 99-102.

"Holiday in Mexico," _Time_, XLVIII (September 2, 1946), 92.

"How to Finance a Movie," _Time_, LI (April 19, 1948), 100-104.

"Ideal Woman," _Time_,XLII(December 20, 1943), 154-58.

"Ivy," _Time_, L (July 7, 1947), 66-68.

"Leading Man," _Time_, LI (January 12, 1948), 52-56.

"A Mother's Tale," _Harper's Bazaar_, LXXXVI (July 1952), 66-68; 102-107.

"The New Pictures," _Time_, XLII (September 20, 1943), 94-96.

"The New Pictures," _Time_, XLIII (March 27, 1944), 94-96.

"The New Pictures," _Time_, XLIV (December 25, 1944), 44-48.

"The New Pictures," _Time_, XLV (January 22, 1945), 91-92.

"The New Pictures," _Time_, XLIX (February 3, 1947), 93-95.

"The New Pictures," _Time_, XLIX (February 24, 1947),106-110.

"The New Pictures," _Time_, XLIX (March 10, 1947), 97-98.

"The New Pictures," _Time_, XLV (April 30, 1947), 89-91.

"The New Pictures," _Time_, LI (February 16, 1948), 99-101.

"The New Pictures," _Time_, LI (March 17, 1948), 102-106.

"The New Pictures," _Time_, LI (March 29, 1948), 98-102.

"The New Pictures," _Time_, LI (May 17, 1948), 102-106.

"The New Pictures," _Time_, LI (May 24, 1948), 96-100.

"The New Pictures," _Time_, LI (September 13, 1948), 102-106.

"The New Pictures," _Time_, LII (November 8, 1948), 102-106.

"Objective Burma," Time, XLV (February 26, 1945), 92-94.

"Old Master," Time, LI (September 20, 1948), 94-100.

"People's Avengers," Time, XLIV (July 10, 1944), 94-96.

"The Postman Always Rings Twice," Time, XLVII (May 6,1946), 96-100.

"Relative Anonymity," Time, LII (August 9, 1948), 74-78.

"Religion and the Intellectuals," Partisan Review, XVII (February 1950), 106-113.

"Report on Italy," Time, XLV (March 5, 1945), 91-92.

"Shoeshine," Time, L (September 8, 1947), 99-100.

"Six Days at Sea," Fortune, XVI (September 1937), 117.

"Street of Chance," Time, XL (December 21, 1942), 100.

"To the Shores of Iwo Jima," Time, XLV (March 26, 1945), 91-96.

"The U.S. Commercial Orchid," Fortune, XII (December 1935), 108.

"The Virginian," Time, XLVII (April 29, 1946), 94-96.

"Watch on the Rhine," Time, XLIII (September 6, 1943), 94-96.

"Wilson," Time, XLIV (August 7, 1944), 84-86.

"With the Marines at Tarawa," Time, XLIII (March 20, 1944), 94.

II. SECONDARY SOURCES

Adler, Renata. "If You Enjoy It, It's Good Enough," New York Times, March 17, 1968, pp. D1; D7.

"Agee on Film: Review and Comments," New Yorker, XXXIV (December 13, 1958), 215.

Aldridge, Leslie. "Who's Afraid of the Undergraduate?" The New York Times Magazine, February 18, 1968, p. D15.

Alpert, Hollis. *The Dreams and the Dreamers*. New York, Macmillan, 1962.

Alpert, Hollis. "Offbeat Director in Outer Space," *The New York Times*, January 16, 1966, pp. 14-15; 40-51.

Arnheim, Rudolf. *Film as Art*. Berkeley, University of California Press, 1957.

"Art of Light and Lunacy: The New Underground Films." Anon. rev., *Time*, February 17, 1967, pp. 94-95.

Balázs, Béla. *Theory of the Film*. trans. Edith Bone. New York, A.N. Roy Publishers, 1953.

Barnouw, Erik, and Krishnaswamy, S. *Indian Film*. New York, Columbia University Press, 1963.

Bart, Peter. "Doesn't Anyone Love a Writer?" *The New York Times*, March 6, 1966, p. xii.

Behar, Jack, "James Agee: The World of His Work." Unpublished dissertation, Ohio State University, 1963.

Bergman, Ingmar. *Four Screenplays of Ingmar Bergman*. New York, Simon and Schuster, 1960.

Bluestone, George. *Novels Into Film*. Berkeley, University of California Press, 1966.

Buñuel, Luis. "A Statement," in *Film Makers on Film Making*. ed. Harry M. Geduld. Bloomington, Indiana University Press, 1967.

Callenbach, Ernest. "Looking Backward," *Film Quarterly*, XXII (Fall 1968), 1-10.

Clair, René. *Reflections on the Cinema*. trans. Vera Traill. London, Kimber, 1953.

Cocteau, Jean. *Diary of a Film*. trans. Roland Duncan. New York, A.W. Roy Publishers, 1950.

Collingwood, R. G. *The Principles of Art*. New York, Oxford University Press, 1961.

Croce, Arlene. "Hollywood the Monolith " *Commonweal*, LXIX (January 23, 1959), 430-433.

Crowther, Bosley. "How Italy Resisted," The New York Times, February 26, 1946, p. 21.

Crowther, Bosley. Review of Agee on Film: Reviews and Comments, American Scholar, XXIX (Summer 1960), 436.

Culahan, Richard. "A Cult Grew Around a Many-Sided Writer," Life, LV (November 1, 1963), 69-72.

Davis, Milton S."'Most Controversial Director'," The New York Times, November 15, 1964, pp.34-35; 104-114.

Eisenstein, Sergei. Film Form and the Film Sense. ed. Jay Leda. Cleveland, World Publishing Company, 1957.

Empson, William. Seven Types of Ambiguity. New York, New Directions, 1958.

"The Eyes Have It," Anon. rev., Time, September 23, 1966, p. 74.

Farber, Manny. "Open City," New Republic, CXV (July 15, 1946), 46.

Farber, Manny. "Star-Gazing for the Middlebrows," New Leader, XLI (December 8, 1958), 14-15.

Farber, Manny. "Underground Films," in Film: An Anthology. ed. Donald Talbot. New York, Simon and Schuster, 1959.

Fiedler, Leslie. "Encounter with Death," New Republic. CXXXVII (December 9, 1957), 25-26.

Film: Book 2, Films of Peace and War. ed. Robert Hughes. New York, Grove Press, Inc., 1962.

Film and Society. ed. Richard Dyer MacCann. New York, Charles Scribner's Sons, 1964.

Fischer, Edward. The Screen Arts. New York, Sheed, 1960.

Frohock, W.M. "James Agee--The Question of Wasted Talent," The Novel of Violence in America. Dallas, Southern Methodist University Press, 1957.

Forster, E. M. Aspects of the Novel. New York, Harcourt Brace Jovanovich, 1954.

Fulton, A.R. Motion Pictures. Oklahoma, University of
    Oklahoma Press, 1960.

Gibbs, Wolcott. "The Kingdom of the Blind," Saturday
    Review of Literature, XXVIII (November 17, 1945),
    7-8.

Gilliatt, Penelope. "On and Off Target," The New Yorker,
    September 7, 1968, pp. 85-88.

Goodman, Ezra. The Fifty Year Decline and Fall of
    Hollywood, New York, MacFadden-Bartell
    Corporation, 1962.

Griffith, Richard. Review of Agee on Film: Reviews and
    Comments, New York Times Book Review, November
    16, 1958, p. 5.

Harker, Jonathan. Review of Agee on Film: Reviews and
    Comments, Film Quarterly, XII (Spring 1959),58-61.

Hatch, Robert. "Olivier's Hamlet," New Republic, CIX,
    (October 4, 1948), 28-30.

Hayes, R. "Rhetoric of Splendor," Commonweal, LXVIII
    (September 12, 1958), 591-92.

Holland, Norman. "Agee on Film: Reviewer Re-Viewed,"
    Hudson Review, XII (Spring 1959), 148-51.

Hopkins, Arthur. "Hamlet and Olivier," Theatre Arts,
    XXXII, (August 1948), 30-31.

Huaco, George A. The Sociology of Film Art, New York,
    Basic Books, 1965.

Hughes, Robert, ed. Film: Book 2, Films of Peace and War.
    New York, Grove Press, Inc., 1962.

Huston, John. "Forward," Agee on Film, Vol. II: Five Film
    Scripts. New York, McDowell Obolensky, 1960.

Jacobs, Lewis, ed. Introduction to the Art of the Movies.
    New York, The Noonday Press, 1960.

James, Henry. "The Art of Fiction," in The House of
    Fiction, Essays on the Novel. ed. Leon Edel.
    London, Greenwood, 1957.

Johnson, William. "Coming to Terms With Color," *Film Quarterly*, XX (Fall 1966), 2-22.

Kael, Pauline. *I Lost It at the Movies*. Boston, Bantam, 1966.

Kael, Pauline. "Movies, The Desperate Art," *Film: An Anthology*, ed. Dan Talbot, Berkeley, University of California Press, 1966.

Kael, Pauline. "That Clean Old Peasant Again," *The New Yorker*, March 2, 1968, pp. 122-128.

Kanter, Stefan. "The Shock of Freedom in Films," *Time*, December 8, 1967, pp. 66-76.

Kauffmann, Stanley. "Life in Reviews," *New Republic*, CXXXIX (December 1, 1958), 18-19.

Kauffmann, Stanley. "Son of a Witch," New Republic, XLVII (June 15, 1968), 26.

Kazin, Alfred. *Contemporaries*. Boston, Little Brown and Co., 1962.

Kerr, Walter. *Criticism and Censorship*. Milwaukee, Bruce Publishing Co., 1954.

Kerr, Walter. *How Not to Write a Play*. New York, Simon and Schuster, 1955.

Knight, Arthur. *The Liveliest Art*. New York, The New American Library, 1957.

Knight, Arthur. Review of *Agee on Film: Reviews and Comments*, *Saturday Review*, XLI (December 20, 1958), 9.

Kozloff, Max. "Le Bonheur," *Film Quarterly*, XX (Winter 1966-67), 35-37.

Kracauer, Siegfried. *From Caligari to Hitler*. Princeton, Princeton University Press, 1947.

Kracauer, Siegfried. *Theory of Film*. New York, Oxford University Press, 1965.

Lester, Elenore. "Shaking the World with an 8-mm. Camera," *The New York Times Magazine*, November 26, 1967, pp. 45-60.

Levin, Meyer. "Abraham Lincoln through the Picture Tube," _Reporter_, VIII (April 14, 1953), 31-33.

Leyda, Jay. "The Pictures are Moving," _New York Times Book Review_, January 2, 1966, pp. 6-7.

Lindgren, Ernest. _The Art of the Film_. New York, Macmillan, 1963.

MacCann, Richard Dyer, ed. _Film: A Montage of Theories_. New York, E. P. Dutton and Co., Inc., 1966.

Macdonald, Dwight. _Against the American Grain_. New York, Random House, 1962.

Macdonald, Dwight. "Agee and the Movies," _Film Heritage_, III (Fall 1967), 3-11.

Macdonald, Dwight. "Chaplin, Verdoux and Agee," _Esquire_, LXIII (April 1965), 18.

Macklin, F. Anthony. "Critic of Honor," _Film Heritage_, III (Fall 1967), 1-2.

Manvell, Roger. _The Film and the Public_. Baltimore, Hunt, Barnard and Co., Ltd., 1955.

Martin, Olga J. _Hollywood's Movie Commandments_. New York, H. W. Wilson Co., 1937.

Mayer, Arthur. "The Parade's Gone By....," _The New York Times_, December 8, 1968, pp.1; 58-60.

McBride, Joseph. "Mr. Macdonald, Mr. Kauffmann and Miss Kael," _Film Heritage_, II (Summer 1967), 26-34.

McCarten, John. "Viva," _New Yorker_, XXII (March 2, 1946), 81.

McLuhan, Marshall. _Understanding Media: The Extensions of Man_. New York, McGraw-Hill, 1964.

Montagu, Ivor. _Film World_. Middlesex, Penguin Books, 1964.

"Not the Best, Not the Worst." Anon. rev., _Time_, March 31, 1967, pp. 92-95.

Oakley, Charles Allen. _Where We Come In_. London, George Allen and Unwin Ltd., 1964.

O'Hara, Shirley. "Chaplin and Hemingway," New Republic, CXIX (May 5, 1947), 34.

Ohlin, Peter Hakan. "James Agee: A Critical Study." Dissertation, University of New Mexico, 1964.

Oulahan, Richard. "A Cult Grew Around a Many-Sided Writer," Life, LV (November 1, 1963), 69-72.

Panofsky, Erwin. "Style and Medium in the Moving Pictures," in Film: An Anthology, ed. Daniel Talbot. New York, Simon and Schuster, 1959.

Phelps, Robert. "James Agee," in The Letters of James Agee to Father Flye. New York, George Braziller, 1962.

Pudovkin, V.I. Film Technique and Film Acting. New York, Grove Press, Inc., 1960.

"Rare Legacy of a Poet," Anon. rev., Life, L (January 27, 1961), 96.

Reed, Rex. "Antonioni: 'After the Blow-Up', a Close-Up," The New York Times, January 1, 1967, p. D7.

Richards, I.A. Principles of Literary Criticism. New York, Harcourt, Brace and World Inc., 1925.

Rotha, Paul. Rotha on the Film. Fair Lawn, Essential Books, 1958.

Schickel, Richard. Movies, the History of an Art and an Institution. New York, Basic Books, 1964.

Scott, Winfield T. Review of Agee on Film: Reviews and Comments, New York Herald Tribune Book Review, February 15, 1959, p. 12.

Sheratsky, Rodney, and Reilly, John L., eds. The Lively Arts. New York, Globe Book Co., 1964.

Siegel, Joel. "On 'Agee on Film'," Film Heritage, III (Fall 1967), 12-19.

Simon, John. "Exemplary Failure," New York Times Book Review, August 14, 1966, p. 24.

Simon, John. "James Agee," Film Heritage, III (Fall 1967), 35.

"Spotlight on Prague," Anon. rev., Newsweek, LXVIII (July 18, 1966), 93-94.

Spottiswoode, Raymond. A Grammar of the Film. Berkeley, University of California Press, 1965.

Stang, Joanne. "'Tis the Season to Be Zinnemann," The New York Times, March 5, 1967, p. D13.

Stephenson, Ralph and Debrix, Jean R. The Cinema as Art. Baltimore, Penguin Books, 1965.

Talbot, Daniel, ed. Film: An Anthology. Berkeley, University of California Press, 1966.

Taylor, John Russell. Cinema Eye, Cinema Ear. New York, Hill and Wong, 1964.

Thorp, Margaret Farrand. America at the Movies. New Haven, Yale University Press, 1939.

Updike, John. "No Use Talking," New Republic, CXLVII (August 13, 1962), 23-24.

Vogel, Amos. "The Onus is Not on the Artist; It Is We Who Must Learn," New York Times, September 11, 1966, p. D15.

Vorkapich, Slavko. "Toward True Cinema," in Introduction to the Art of the Movies, ed. Lewis Jacobs. New York, Noonday Press, 1960.

Wagenknecht, Edward. The Movies in the Age of Innocence. Oklahoma, University of Oklahoma Press, 1962.

Waldron, Gloria. The Information Film. New York, Columbia University Press, 1949.

Weales, Gerald. "The Critic in Love," Reporter, XIX December 25, 1958), 38-39.

White, E. B. and Strunk, William, Jr. The Elements of Style. New York, Macmillan, 1959.

Zalman, Jan. "Question Marks on the Czechoslovak Cinema," Film Quarterly, XXI (Winter 1967-68), 18-27.

Zinsser, Wm. K. Seen Any Good Movies Lately? New York, Doubleday and Co., 1958.

DISSERTATIONS ON FILM

An Arno Press Collection

Beaver, Frank Eugene. **Bosley Crowther**: Social Critic of the Film, 1940-1967. First publication, 1974

Benderson, Albert Edward. **Critical Approaches to Federico Fellini's "8½"**. First publication, 1974

Berg, Charles Merrell. **An Investigation of the Motives for and Realization of Music to Accompany the American Silent Film, 1896-1927**. First publication, 1976

Blades, Joseph Dalton, Jr. **A Comparative Study of Selected American Film Critics, 1958-1974**. First publication, 1976

Bohn, Thomas William. **An Historical and Descriptive Analysis of the "Why We Fight" Series**. First publication, 1977

Cohen, Louis Harris. **The Cultural-Political Traditions and Developments of the Soviet Cinema: 1917-1972**. First publication, 1974

Dart, Peter. **Pudovkin's Films and Film Theory**. First publication, 1974

Davis, Robert Edward. **Response to Innovation**: A Study of Popular Argument about New Mass Media. First publication, 1976

Facey, Paul W. **The Legion of Decency**: A Sociological Analysis of the Emergence and Development of a Social Pressure Group. First publication, 1974

Feldman, Charles Matthew. **The National Board of Censorship (Review) of Motion Pictures, 1909-1922**. First publication, 1977

Feldman, Seth R. **Evolution of Style in the Early Work of Dziga Vertov**. First publication, 1977

Flanders, Mark Wilson. **Film Theory of James Agee**. First publication, 1977

Fredericksen, Donald Laurence. **The Aesthetic of Isolation in Film Theory**: Hugo Munsterberg. First publication, 1977

Gosser, H. Mark. **Selected Attempts at Stereoscopic Moving Pictures and Their Relationship to the Development of Motion Picture Technology, 1852-1903**. First publication, 1977

James, C. Rodney. **Film as a National Art**: NFB of Canada and the Film Board Idea. First publication, 1977

Karimi, A. M. **Toward a Definition of the American Film Noir (1941-1949)**. First publication, 1976

Karpf, Stephen L. **The Gangster Film**: Emergence, Variation and Decay of a Genre, 1930-1940. First publication, 1973

Lounsbury, Myron O. **The Origins of American Film Criticism, 1909-1939**. First publication, 1973

Lyons, Robert J[oseph]. **Michelangelo Antonioni's Neo-Realism:** A World View. First publication, 1976

Lyons, Timothy James, **The Silent Partner:** The History of the American Film Manufacturing Company, 1910-1921. First publication, 1974

McLaughlin, Robert. **Broadway and Hollywood:** A History of Economic Interaction. First publication, 1974

Maland, Charles J. **American Visions:** The Films of Chaplin, Ford, Capra, and Welles, 1936-1941. First publication, 1977

Mason, John L. **The Identity Crisis Theme in American Feature Films, 1960-1969.** First publication, 1977

North, Joseph H. **The Early Development of the Motion Picture, 1887-1909.** First publication, 1973

Paine, Jeffery Morton. **The Simplification of American Life:** Hollywood Films of the 1930's. First publication, 1977

Pryluck, Calvin. **Sources of Meaning in Motion Pictures and Television.** First publication, 1976

Rimberg, John. **The Motion Picture in the Soviet Union, 1918-1952.** First publication, 1973

Sanderson, Richard Arlo. **A Historical Study of the Development of American Motion Picture Content and Techniques Prior to 1904.** First publication, 1977

Sands, Pierre N. **A Historical Study of the Academy of the Motion Picture Arts and Sciences (1927-1947).** First publication, 1973

Shain, Russell Earl. **An Analysis of Motion Pictures about War Released by the American Film Industry, 1939-1970.** First publication, 1976

Snyder, John J. **James Agee:** A Study of His Film Criticism. First publication, 1977

Stuart, Frederic. **The Effects of Television on the Motion Picture and Radio Industries.** First publication, 1976

Wead, George. **Buster Keaton and the Dynamics of Visual Wit.** First publication, 1976

Wolfe, Glenn J. **Vachel Lindsay:** The Poet as Film Theorist. First publication, 1973